Soul Primer

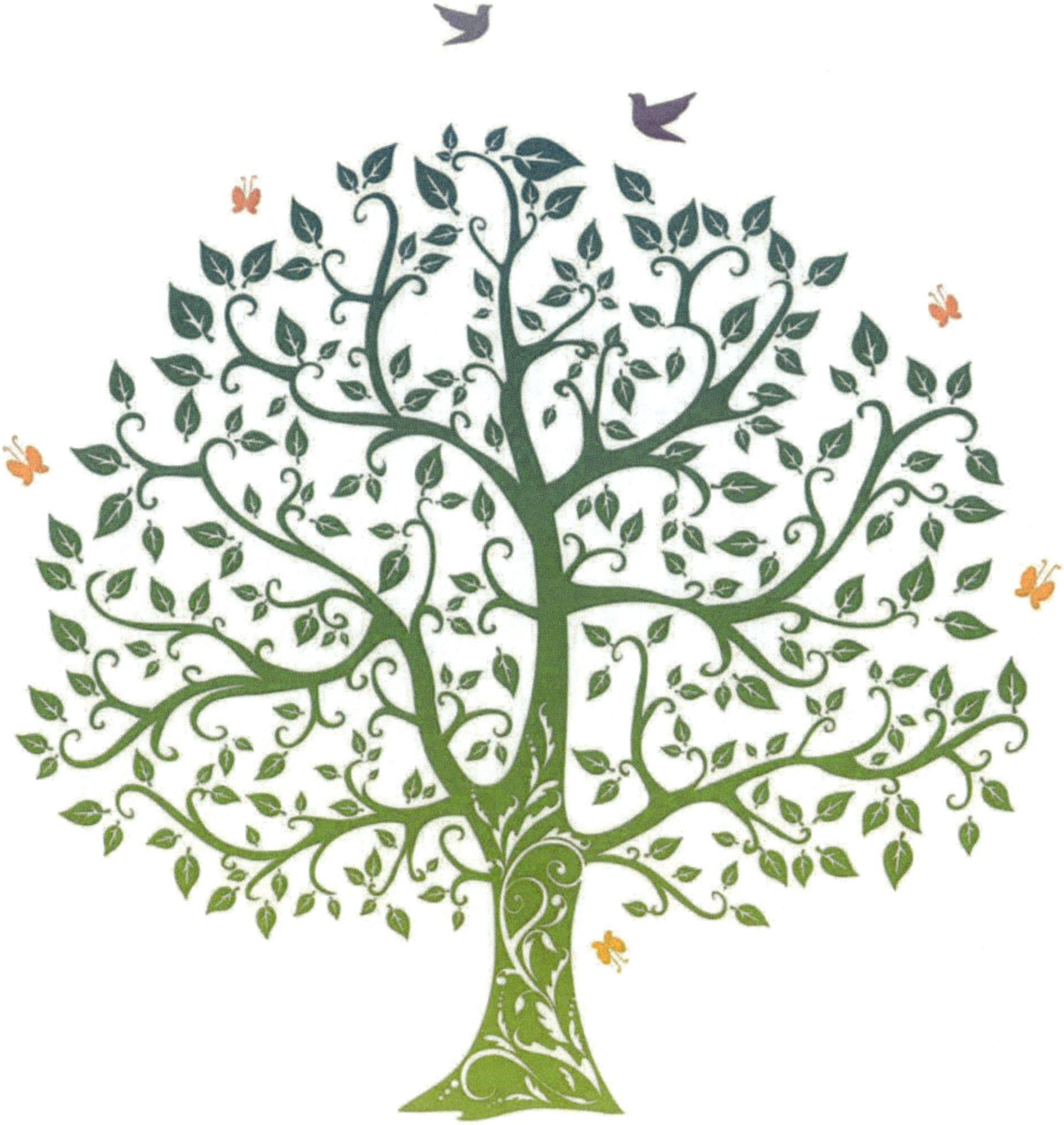

Soul Primer

A Spiritual Alphabet for the Soul

Text by
CATE SCHULTZ

Art by
SUSAN COHEN THOMPSON
JUDITH SHAW
JACK GUNTER

Letters and Doodles by
SUSAN COHEN THOMPSON

Photography by
CATE SCHULTZ

Cover art by
JUDITH SHAW

Acknowledgments

For the unconditional love I have been blessed with, I am eternally grateful.

I especially recognize my mother, Rita Joan Schultz "The Saint" for being such a role model for compassion, love, and patience.

I also thank my sons, Bryce "Clever Tiger," John "Brave Bear," and Kennan "Dancing Leaves," for always loving me "Soaring Heart," no matter what....

To these human loves, I acknowledge the amazing and powerful love and care of the Universe. Time and again, pearls of wisdom, unexpected sources of financial support, and intuitive knowing have been gifted to me as the blessings of walking in divine spirit.

Finally, a huge shout out to my beloved partner, Dave Mills, who loved, supported, and fed me even when I seemed lost, deep in the meditating and birthing of this new creation from the womb of the Universe.

INTRODUCTION
2
HOW TO USE *SOUL PRIMER*
4
PREFACE
5-6
UNSPOKEN PRAYER
8
THE AWAKENING
9
SPIRITUAL ALPHABET
10-112
I AM BEAUTIFUL
21
NAMASTE
41
LOVING KINDNESS PRAYER
49
A MEDITATION DREAM
57
SHE BECAME THE SKY
61
IT IS HERE THAT I DWELL
73
RESOURCE PAGES/WORKSHEETS
113-122
AFTERWARD
123-124
ABOUT THE AUTHOR
125-126
ABOUT THE ARTISTS
127-132
THE IMPOSSIBLE DREAM
133

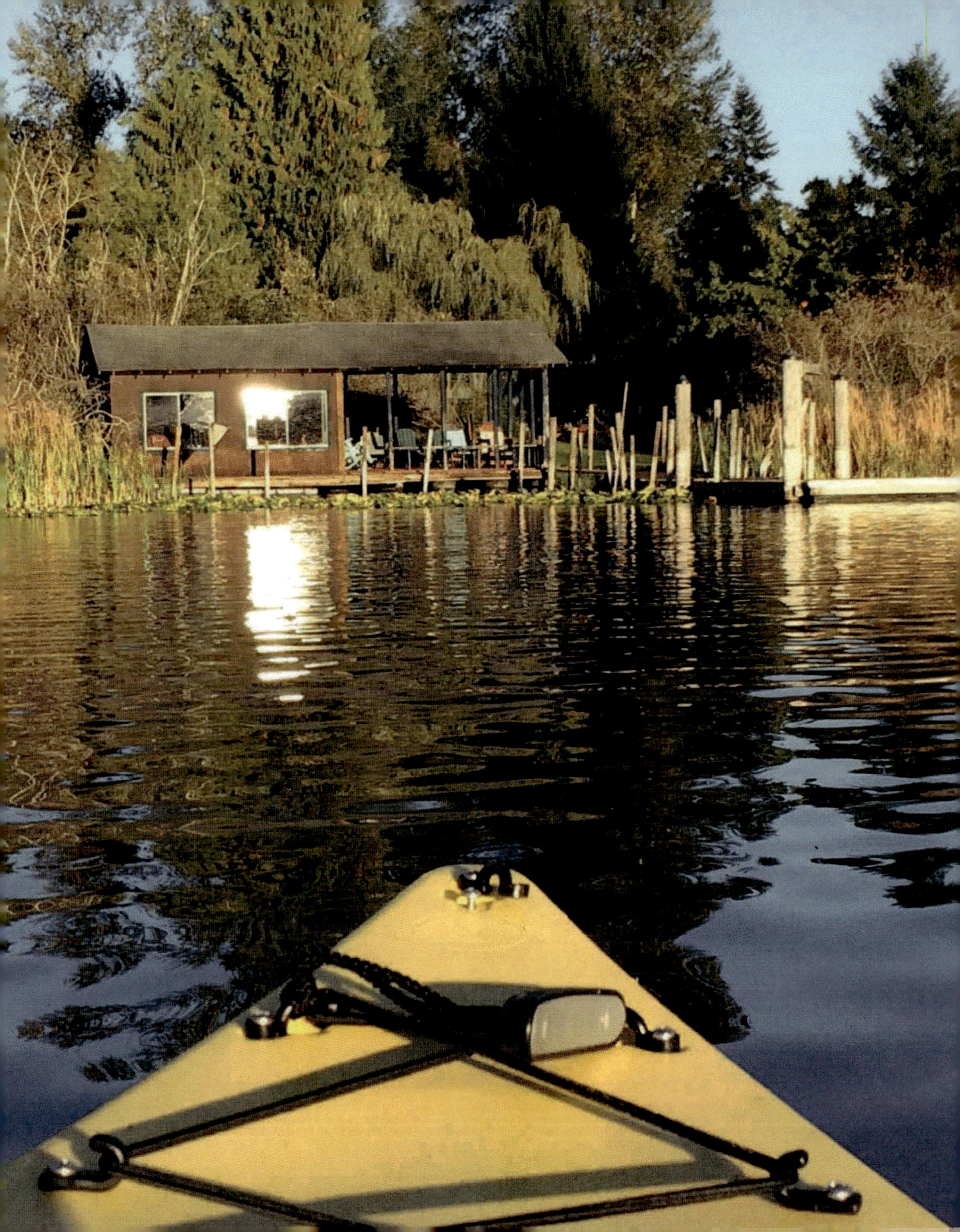

Introduction

The world, as we know it, is rapidly changing. There is a paradigm shift happening that is accelerating the evolution of the human species. People are moving away from the old ways of darkness. We are becoming aware that the foods and pills and beliefs fostered by ignorance, advertising, and greed are killing us. Deep down, we know there is a better way. We see examples of people who seem to have figured it out, who have somehow become enlightened. They don't seem to work as hard, or suffer as much, as others. They're healthier. Their eyes are brighter. They make it look easy to achieve amazing things. What do they know that we don't?

You've heard the buzzwords: *Abundance, Presence, Intuition.* You've heard the advice: *Meditate to manage stress; Gratitude is the key to happiness; Learn to be one with the Universe.* There are so many things to do, and lots of books on how to do them. Yet, most of us are just trying to make it through the workday, and family commitments, so we can fall into bed at night and sleep long enough to be ready to do it again the next day. When we do find time to read, we want an escape, not 200 pages on Inner Peace or Compassion - although the gorgeous books that focus on these valuable concepts are treasures for those who have time for them.

Soul Primer is a guide for the busy person who wants to learn, in easy steps, how to get started on - or expand upon - the path to personal growth. With one easy concept per week, you will develop an awareness and working knowledge of skills that can lead to a regular practice for creating and sustaining a more healthy, fulfilled, rewarding life.

If you already have some of these spiritual life skills, use this book as a luscious reminder and refresher of the nourishment needed to feed a soul. Be open to new growth as it comes.

If you are ready to find a better way to live, now is the time to begin the practices outlined in *Soul Primer*. Every week, read one letter of the alphabet and enjoy the heart-opening art. Easy exercises will help you focus on the weekly concept and guide you on how to fit it into your regular life. Only one page to read each week! Directing your life to a better path, and a brighter place, is an ongoing process. *Soul Primer* makes it simple, straightforward, beautiful, and fun!

Make this the day that you step into the life you have always wanted. The secret to creating miracles in your life is creating daily habits that support your personal growth. Start today to learn the skills that are revolutionizing mankind. Change is happening fast. Be a part of the change, for your own good, and for the good of our world.

It's as easy as A, B, C.

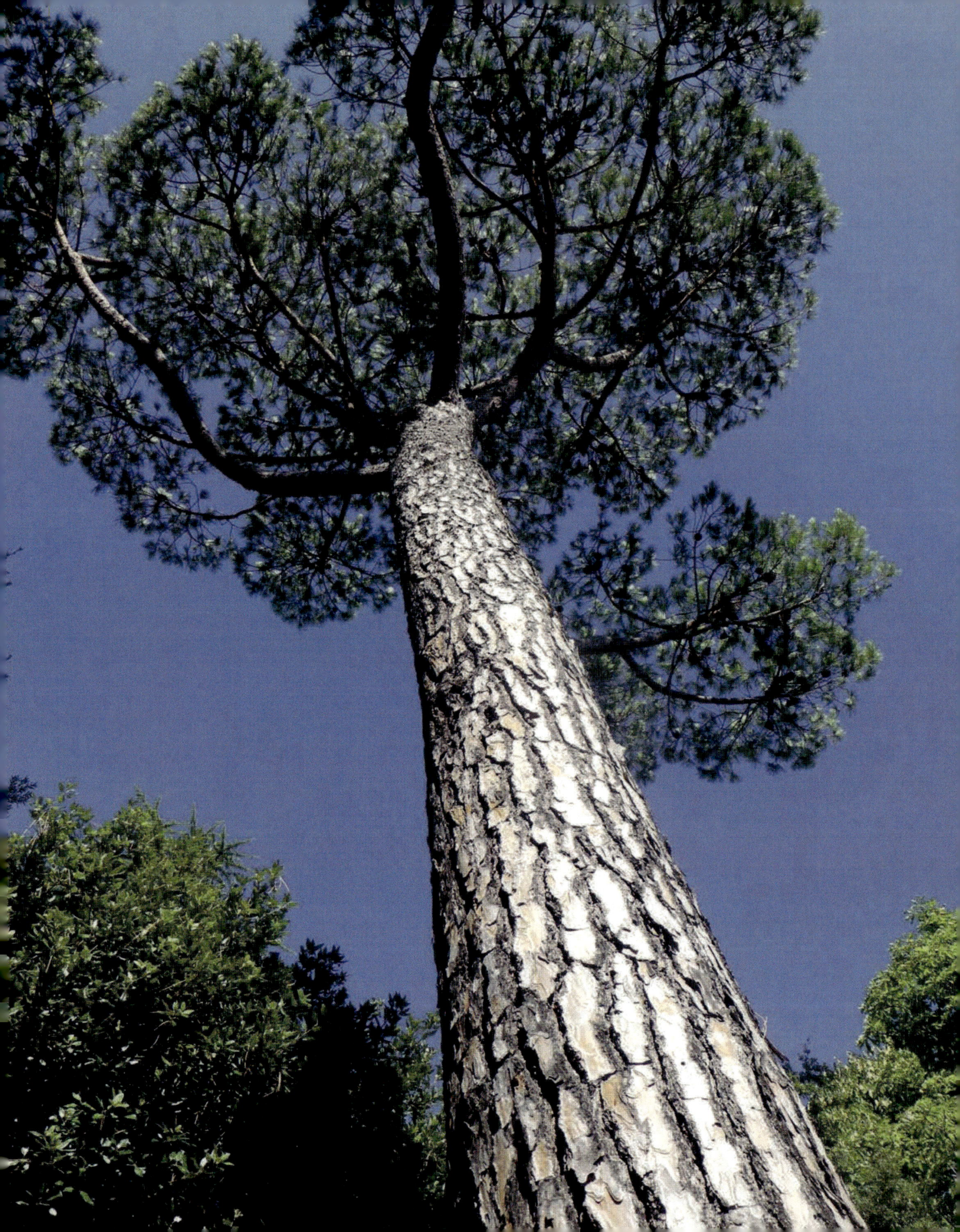

How to use *Soul Primer*

This easy and beautiful book will guide you through 26 weeks of life-changing practices.

Each week, a new idea is introduced, followed by a simple way to exercise the concept. Copy the week's *Daily Reminder* to a place where you can see it easily and say it aloud at least once a day. Practice the concept for a week and make notes in your journal on your experiences. Finally, the *Ongoing Goal* guides you to continuing the practice on a regular basis.

Although it may be tempting to fast-track the book, I encourage you to take only one weekly concept at a time. Taking the full week to focus on each idea allows it to settle and grow in your spirit, bringing new possibilities up from within. Even if you "already know" a concept, use that week as a reminder. Refreshing our awareness helps us stay "in tune" and deepens our understanding of a practice. Be open to new insights from the Universe.

You may go through the book in order, from A to Z, or you may randomly choose a different letter each week. Either approach is fine. If you prefer random selection, find a way to mark the pages you have already studied so you can make it through the book in 26 weeks. You may want to go through *Soul Primer* in alphabetical order for six months and then repeat for another six months, choosing pages at random. *Soul Primer* is a guidebook that can be used again and again.

Each page of artwork has been created by artists to contribute to the beauty of your experience and to inspire additional awakenings in your soul.

Please purchase or make a journal to accompany your *Soul Primer* journey. Have it with you as you study and practice each concept. Writing thoughts or drawing images about your experiences is key to fully understanding and absorbing, not just the ideas, but your relationship to them and their relationship to your life. Savor the path and be an appreciative observer of the moment.

Finally, don't be too serious about the process! Be kind to yourself and open to your experience. Some concepts may feel more natural, or come easily; others may be more challenging. I guarantee that every one of them, when adopted as a life habit, will improve your experience here on earth. All of these practices are appropriate and beneficial for any person, no matter what religion, social position, economic standing, or walk of life.

I can say, with confidence and experience, that focusing on these weekly concepts and adopting them into your routine will change your life. It takes 21 days to create a habit. As you progress, try to maintain awareness of the previous weeks' teachings and continue to apply them forward as much as possible. Soon, you will see your life blossoming into one of beauty and grace.

Many Blessings on your journey!

Preface

I created *Soul Primer* to provide the skill set often missing in our lives, skills we may never have been taught.

People come to me wanting help with specific problems, such as how to handle sadness or anger or resentment. Maybe they are having problems with their boss, spouse, or child. Maybe they cannot find love or motivate themselves toward a goal.

These are all valid problems and there are tools and tricks to manage them, such as count to 10, make goal sheets, channel an archetype, take a pill, etc.

Yet, underlying these current or temporary issues is always a lack of fundamental skills.

Imagine you are in charge of building a house
you must occupy
for the rest of your days.

Any carpenter would tell you that you need certain skills and tools to do a good job: You need to be able to measure accurately. You need to be able to use a saw to cut wood. You need to be able to hammer a nail in straight and use a level, often while balancing on a ladder. You need to be able to mix concrete, install plumbing, do electrical wiring, lay roofing, attach insulation, and texture a wall. There are so many things involved in building a house correctly.

Now imagine you tried to build a house without these skills. Before long, you would need to call for help to fix the crumbling foundation, or the dripping pipes, or the leaning chimney. The house would be drafty and maybe even dangerous, if the gas pipes leaked or the furnace was installed improperly. You could spend the rest of your life hiring people to fix the doors that don't close properly or the windows that weren't set correctly, or the fuse breakers that constantly blow.

Obviously, it would be beneficial to have the tools to do a better job. After all, this is the house you need to live in for the rest of your life.

Now, imagine you are in charge of building a life
you must occupy
for the rest of your days.

As with building a house, a certain skill set is required to execute the job well. Having these skills, or tools, would save you the necessity of calling in experts to help fix things that go wrong.

Some of us may get lucky and have great parents or teachers or mentors that taught us the skills we need to build a life. Unfortunately, this is not always the case and, indeed, our parents and teachers are just doing the best they can with what *they* were given, which may have been inadequate.

We are taught to read and add two plus two, but we are not taught soul skills. Without these basics, we find ourselves having to hire people (therapists, counselors, coaches) to fix the things that are not working properly.

Soul Primer teaches the skills, and provides the tools, to build a trouble-free life. Just as we learn the basic building blocks of the alphabet in order to read well, we must learn the basic building blocks of the spirit in order to live well.

In *Soul Primer,* I took critical life skills and distilled them down to their essential drops, much like a scientist boils saltwater down, down, down until just the salt is left. I tried not to waste a single word along the way. Are these quick fixes? Yes and no. You can make great progress, and have huge awakenings, in one week. Then, if a concept resonates with you, I encourage you to pursue it further through sources easily found on the internet.

Living from the soul is a joyful, life-long journey that benefits not only you, but all those around you and, indeed, the world at large. *Soul Primer* introduces the skills in a concise and easy format; it is up to you to take these tools and use them. *Soul Primer* raises your awareness; it is up to you to commit to applying that awareness to your life.

Start today to become an expert in building
the life of your dreams.

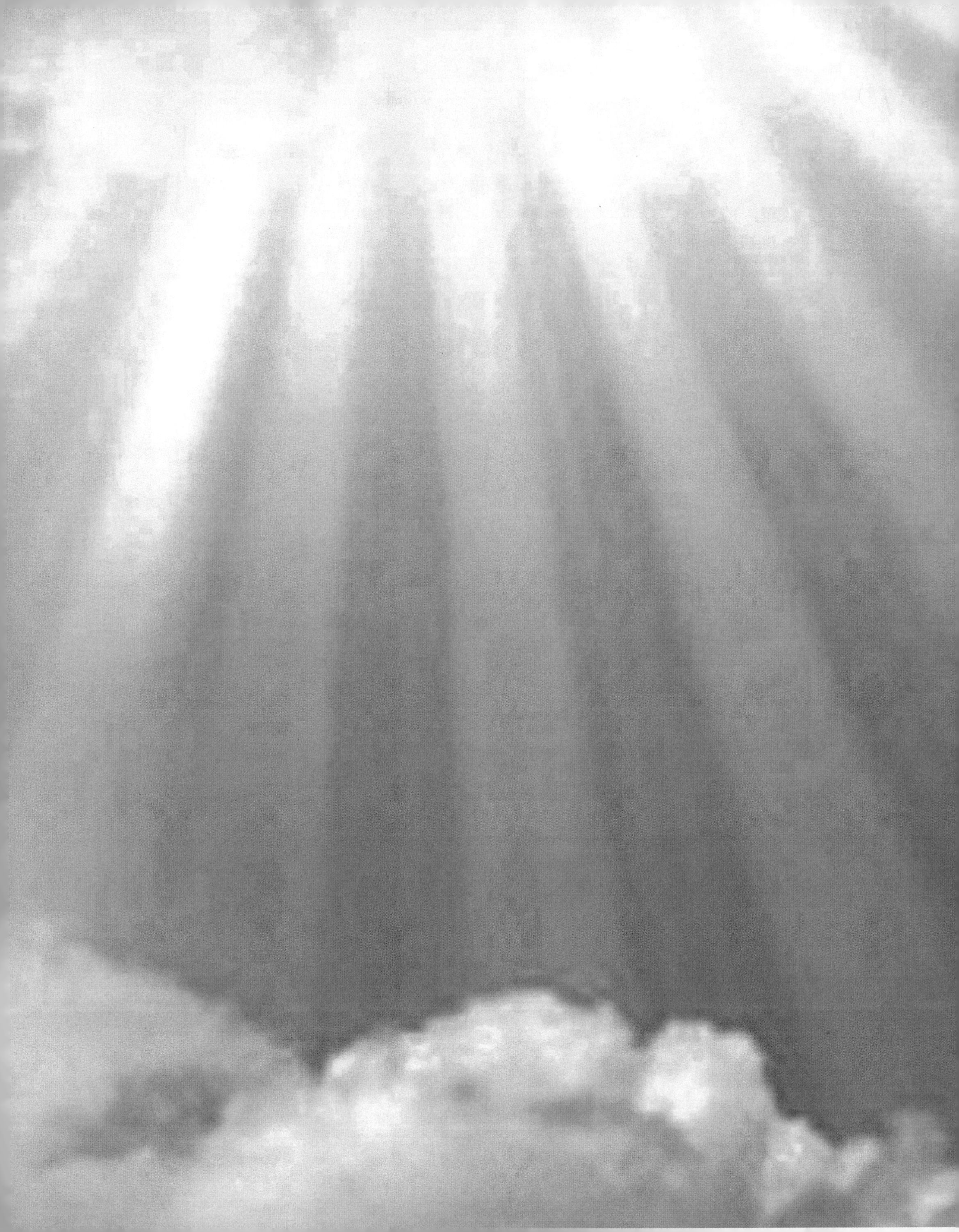

Unspoken Prayer

There is a place,
in the hours before dawn,
where souls fly on night winds
and truth shines down in starlight.

An unspoken prayer hangs
on that midnight breeze,
like a mirage in the mist
of human emotion,
and for a moment,
on bended knee,
one knows the heart of god.

And neither to the left,
nor to the right,
nor above or below,
lie the answers,
but, rather, deep within you,
in your own heart,
in the heaven of god's eye,
where the clouds
of fear,
and friends' opinions,
and restraints of time or space,
disappear beyond the horizon.

It is there,
written in the eternal sky,
to go forth,
in your own unique greatness
and create a perfect light
out of the beauty and love
that is you,
and you alone.

Cate Schultz

The letter "A" is symbolic of new beginnings
.
Many alphabets begin with the letter "A," including English("A"), Hebrew("Aleph"), Greek ("Alpha"), Arabic ("Aliph"), and Latin ("A").

A is also the beginning of the sacred words Amen and Ameen, as well as the first sound of AUM
(known to most westerners as "Om").

AUM is the most ancient and sacred mantra in Hinduism.
It is the primordial sound, the hymn of the universe, associated with cosmic sound, mystical syllable,
divine affirmation.
It is the ultimate vibration that contains every vibration, like white light contains every color.
AUM is the white light of sound.

The first vibration of the AUM, the "A," stands for Akara, the creation, beginning, or waking stage.

May this Soul Primer be a beginning, an awakening, a creation of a greater you.
If you have already begun, may this book help you begin again.
And again.
May every day, and every moment, be a new beginning of a new waking as, week by week, you expand your being into a beautiful new awareness of light and love.

With Blessings and Love,
Cate

Week One

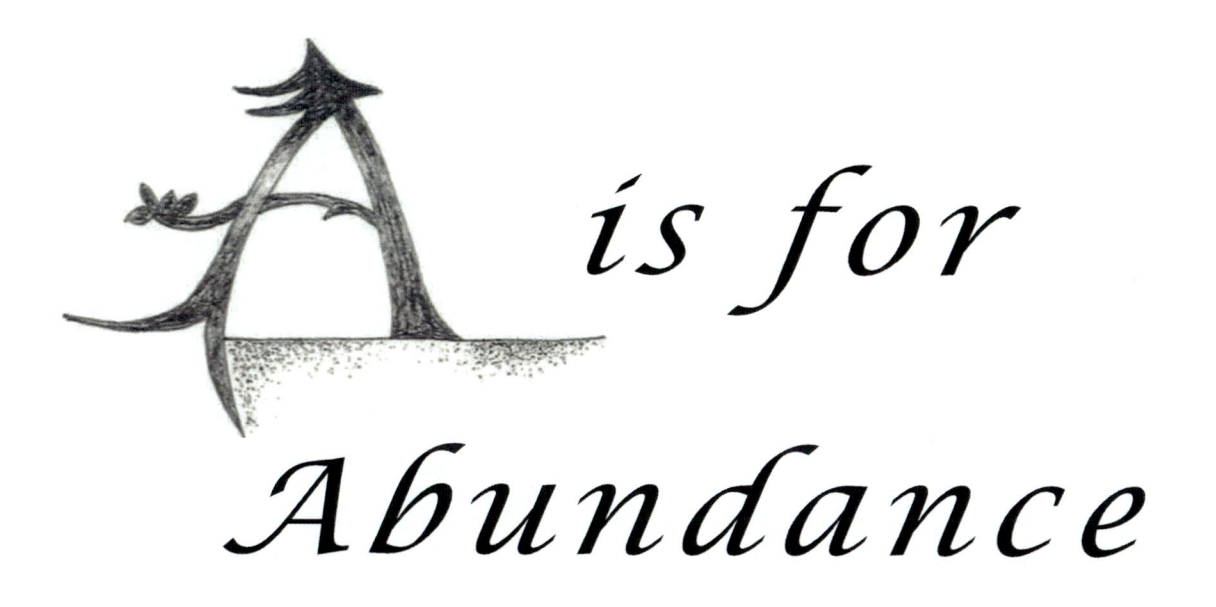

A is for Abundance

Daily Reminder

"I appreciate the abundance already present in my life and view every situation as an opportunity to welcome more abundance."

Abundance is yours to declare

Abundance is like a lottery ticket you have already won, you just need to claim it. Abundance is not waiting for you to land a better job or manifest a nicer car. It is yours already; you simply need to recognize it.

Start by banishing the belief that abundance has to do with how much money/food/toys you have. There are miserable rich people, and people that lead simple lives with great joy. It is not about having a lot to be happy; it is about being happy to have a lot.

Eckart Tolle says, ***"Acknowledging the good in your life is the foundation for all abundance."*** We do this by seeing and appreciating what we already have, *in every situation*. Are you stuck in traffic? Say, "I am so fortunate to not be the one in an accident right now!" Is your co-worker ruining your day? Say, "I sure am lucky to have a paying job!" Is it raining? Say, "What a blessing this life-giving water is to our world." Is your alarm clock your worst enemy? Watch daylight unfurl across the night sky and say, "How wonderful that I get to see another day!" Did you mess up somewhere in life, miss out on an opportunity, maybe experience hurt or sadness? As hard as it may be, say aloud, "I am blessed to have situations in my life that help me to grow and evolve." Your journey is rich or poor based on your perception.

As you practice focusing on the blessing of *every part* of your life, no matter how mundane or undesirable it may seem, abundance will begin to multiply. As you become convinced that you are lucky, fortunate, blessed, and rich, so you will be. By being more aware and present to your existing abundance, you raise your energy frequency to a higher level. And like attracts like. Your glowing abundance will attract people and situations that build more abundance.

Start today to create a life of abundance by becoming acutely aware and appreciative of the abundance that already surrounds you.

This Week:

Set aside 2 minutes each morning, afternoon, and evening to pause and recognize abundance. Sink full of dishes? Say, "I am so lucky to have food to eat!" Rent due? Look around and say, "I am fortunate to not have to live under a bridge." Got a cold? Direct love to your amazing body for fighting off intruders. At first it may seem fake but, with practice, abundance will build in your life. Soon, recognition of the abundance all around you will come more easily, and will begin to attract more and more abundance to you. Record your observations in your journal.

Ongoing Goal:

Write the word ABUNDANCE somewhere prominent and remind yourself daily to find examples of how abundant your life is. With regular practice, you will see abundance multiply in your life.

The merit of a human is
not visible with the eyes,
but shines like a beacon
to the spirit.
See with your spirit,
not your eyes.
-Cate Schultz

Week Two

B *is for*

Beauty

Daily Reminder

"I see beyond a person's physical attributes and recognize the beauty that lies within each of us."

Learn to see Beauty

There is truth in the saying, "Beauty is in the eye of the Beholder." Although this maxim is generally used to indicate that beauty is subjective, and that visual colors, shapes, and forms appeal to each of us differently, it can also be flipped on its head to help us understand where beauty begins: Beauty begins in us; it is not out there; it is in us, the Beholder. We create beauty in our mind's eye. When we train our eye to behold beauty in everyone, regardless of color, shape, or form, then the world becomes more beautiful.

We learn to see beauty in everyone by first acknowledging that our modern concept of beauty is flawed. Our culture, through magazine covers, media, movies, etc., has taught us to judge beauty based on physical attributes. However, our bodies are just vessels and the good stuff really lies within. We know that putting fine wine in a plain jar, or putting contaminated water in an elegant pitcher, doesn't change the quality of the contents. Likewise, our external bodies are not an indication of what lies inside. Know, once and for all, that true beauty lies in the sacred spirit that abides in each of us. Recognize that every human body, no matter its shape or form, is just a vessel that eventually will be turned to dust. Look beyond the external appearance and see the beauty of the divine spirit within, which, according to anecdotal evidence, appears to continue on in some way when its human shell expires.

Remember, too, that each of us begins as a perfect, untarnished being. Over time, and exposure to suffering, that perfect being may develop layers that occlude its luminescence. Yet, even people who are damaged or broken, from abuse, mistreatment, neglect, drugs, or other degrading inputs, are still perfect souls. Like a gold nugget covered with mud, the treasure is still there. Some people have learned to cleanse themselves of the muddy layers with tools like those found in this book. Others have not. Regardless of how tarnished a soul may seem, know that underneath lies a perfect spirit. It is that eternal, cosmic soul we honor with the recognition of beauty.

Start today to see, with love, the inner beauty of everyone you meet. BE a Beholder of Beauty.

<u>This Week:</u>

Make a conscious walk, each day, where you observe every single person you encounter with "eyeglasses of love." This walk could be in a mall, down the hall at your workplace, at the grocery store, or anywhere you choose. Look at each person you pass and consciously disregard their physical condition. See them as if they are a beautiful soul, because they are. Beneath the layers they carry from this world's wounds, they are unique, beautiful, precious manifestations of life. Record your observations in your journal.

Ongoing Goal:

Remind yourself that outer appearance is not an indication of value. Regularly wear those x-ray eyeglasses of love, like a pair of real glasses, to see the inside beauty of all humans.

You can't use up creativity. The more you use, the more you have.
    -Maya Angelou

Week Three

C is for Creativity

Daily Reminder

"I practice being curious and aware, while changing it up and not worrying about what others think."

Creativity makes life juicy

Many of us believe we are not creative. We don't think we can act/paint/write/invent/sing. We believe creativity is the playground of artists and geniuses who possess a special gift. Yet, we all came into this world with creative capacities, unique to us alone. Creativity is simply curiosity pursued, and not bound by fear. Exercising creativity is like going from dull and gray to bright and colorful. We can learn to coax out the creativity that may have been stifled in us at an early age.

The first step is to become curious, to wonder at things. Instead of squashing a bug, stop to admire its iridescent colors and fuzzy legs. Listen to the song it makes with its wings. *Be curious.*

The second step is to become aware, in a child-like way, of your world. Learn to see things consciously. When Van Gogh painted the night sky, or Cezanne painted apples, or Whistler painted his mother, they stopped and looked, for a very long time, at their subjects. When was the last time you stopped to really gaze at apples? When have you consciously noted the gentle slope of your mother's back? How about the gold speckles in your child's eyes? Stop. Look. Notice. *Be aware.*

The third step is to boldly change it up, whatever "it" is. Creativity comes in many forms. Chicken again for dinner? Try a new combination of flavors. Driving the kids to school? Make a rap song out of it. Another meeting? Start it with a haiku challenge. The point is simply to open the gates to creative expression. Life is too precious to waste on mundane living. Adding creative expression to everyday activities makes the mundane magnificent! *Change it up* and add sparkle to your day!

The fourth step is to not worry about what others think. Every realized creator has had to get past the fear of their art/idea being rejected or ridiculed. Fortunately, history is full of people who ignored others' negative opinions and persevered into fame. Perish the idea that anyone's approval is required for you to sing loudly, dance alone, photograph grass, fling paint, weld junk, stack rocks, or whatever it is that moves you. Do it your way and *don't worry* about what others think.

Start today to exercise your creativity and watch your life grow more joyful and fun.

This Week:

Each morning, decide ahead on a routine task that you will do a little differently today. Either plan or improvise on the spot how you will change it up. Add humor, paints, music, poetry, play dough at will. Write about the experience in your journal.

Ongoing Goal:

Continue to work on your skills of really looking at the people, situations, and things in your life. Each day, turn at least one observation or event into a creative endeavor, no matter how simple or complex.

I am a beautiful,
divine soul with immense power.
I am a spirit on a journey that
cannot be contained.
I am whole and healed from the
traumas and wounds of this life.
My powers are being called
and I can no longer play small.
-Cate Schultz

Week Four

D is for Divinity

Daily Reminder

"The god-presence of the universe lives in me, providing power, light, and clarity."

Remember your Divinity

Recognizing the divine within us is an integral part of our personal journey and the basis of the spiritual revolution sweeping our world. Every religion refers to the god-presence within us and even science is realizing that we are more than just biological creatures. De Chardin said, *"We are not human beings having a spiritual experience. We are spiritual beings having a human experience."* And from Carl Sagan: *"The cosmos is within us. We are made of star-stuff."* Call it what you will, there is an energy that runs through us all. Rumi says, *"You are not a drop in the ocean, you are the entire ocean in a drop."* Here are scientists, poets, and philosophers telling us the same thing. We are cosmic. We are spirit. We are the universe. We are divine.

Most of us have forgotten our divine spirit. We get carried away by the jumble of life. We burn away our lives doing jobs we hate; we stifle frivolous creative urges; we accumulate things in an effort to find happiness; we hoard possessions to protect us from our fears; we destroy our earth and our brothers and sisters because we believe in scarcity. Our fears and insecurities create a recurring cycle of suffering. We have forgotten our divinity, individually and collectively.

Change starts with you. You must remember your divine nature so that you can begin to live by its illumination and be able to shine the light for others. Your divine self is your highest self, it is the essence of the universe that dwells within you. Your divine self is connected to the source of all light and life and it is where your true power abides.

Start today to recognize your own divinity.

This Week:

Set aside ten minutes each morning for this important work. Sit in a quiet place, eyes closed, and become aware of your breathing. Breathe in and out several times, focusing on your breath. Set your intention by saying silently or aloud:

I release any thoughts or beliefs that are obstacles to connecting with my divine self.
I am open to the guidance and light of my divine self and the power of the universe in me.

You may ask for specific guidance or insight, or just open yourself to receiving light and love. Imagine light flowing into you through the top of your head and slowly filling every part of your body. Rest quietly as you become infused with light energy. Be open to the experience. You may feel an answer, or just feel peaceful. Regardless of how you feel, know that contact has been made. Regularly connecting with your divine self will open the communication channels and you will begin to see wonderful inspirations arise from this openness. Write or draw about your experiences and reactions in your journal.

Ongoing Goal:

Commit to practicing every letter of *Soul Primer*, for a week and for a lifetime. At the end of six months, you will be well on your way to living in the power of your own divinity.

Crazy last thought: You are a creature of divine light and love, temporarily inhabiting a human body. Are you taking good care of the vessel that holds such precious cargo? Cherish your body, not for how it looks, but for how it carries your soul through this world.

> You can only understand people if you feel them in yourself.
>
> — John Steinbeck

Week Five

E is for Empathy

Daily Reminder

"I cannot know all that a person has been through, but I can take the time to consider and feel their experience in a way that builds empathy for all."

Empathy connects us to others

Empathy enables us to feel another's emotions, whether positive or negative. All of us could benefit from the practice of relating to others' experiences.

Empathy involves imagining what a person is going through and mentally putting ourselves in the same situation to see how it might feel. This is more than just sending a sympathy card to someone who is grieving. This is stopping to look at the dirty homeless man and to imagine what it feels like to sleep on a cold sidewalk under a tattered tarp. This is stopping to really see the elderly woman walking so darn slow in front of you and to imagine what it feels like to have the aches and pains of an aged body. This is stopping to watch the child who is interrupting your peace with his running and boisterous shouts and to imagine what it feels like to have such carefree joy.

Empathy is the skill of relating to others and it requires stopping: stopping our inclination to rush past; stopping our impulse to judge; stopping to just breathe and really feel the human condition. It may not be comfortable to look into another's experience and try to feel their emotions but learning to do so will create healing in your life, in your relationships, and in the world at large.

Empathy in action (compassion) is when your awareness of others' experience leads you to do something for them, whether it be as small as a smile or a kind word, or as big as a gift of time or money. Or simply a silent blessing that you send out to them from your heart. The practice of compassion has been shown to benefit others, and to increase our own well-being. Empathy and compassion, like so many skills, grow with practice.

Start today to practice empathy as the first step toward living with compassion for all creatures.

This Week:

Once each day, take the time to "walk in the shoes" of a fellow being, whether someone you know, or a stranger. Notice, particularly, if you catch yourself feeling irritated or impatient or judgmental and try to stop, take a deep breath, and remind yourself that you cannot know another's path in entirety. Ask yourself, "I wonder what their life is like? I wonder what it is like to be them?" "I wonder what kind of childhood they had, and what chain of events brought them to this place?" Take the time, without rushing, to really feel what they may be feeling. If possible, move into compassion and send them a silent blessing.
Record your thoughts and experiences in your journal.

Ongoing Goal:

Continue to practice random acts of empathy and conscious acts of compassion until they become regular habits. Being aware and mindful of our shared human experience contributes to healing, both personal and global.

"Aren't you afraid of dying?"
she was asked.

"I'm more afraid of not living,"
she replied.

Week Six

F is for Fearlessness

Daily Reminder

"I set aside imagined fears and step boldly into the challenges and adventures of a fulfilled life"

Fearlessness opens the doors and windows of your life

Learning to be fearless requires ascertaining the validity of our fears and evaluating the consequences of allowing those fears to govern us.

Fears can be simplified into two categories: real and present dangers (i.e. a tiger running at us) and imagined fears (things that "might" happen to us). Things like fear of failure, fear of rejection, fear of being alone, fear of making a mistake, fear of what people will think, fear of getting sick or hurt, etc., are all imagined fears.

The first step in facing fears is to ask yourself, "Is this a real and present danger?" Emphasis is on the "present" factor. There are many things that *might* be dangerous, and yet can be done safely (driving a car, flying an airplane, climbing a mountain). Unless the danger is imminent and requires immediate action for survival, it is an imagined fear.

The second step is to envision yourself sitting on a rocking chair in your old age and looking back on your life. Are you wondering, with regret, what might have happened if you started that business, took that trip, asked that boy out, wrote that book, made that speech, started that project, climbed that mountain? Or are you chuckling at the adventures you had as you bravely faced your fears down and stepped forward courageously into life? We all have fears. Fears are a natural protective instinct left from prehistoric times. We can hide meekly behind them, or acknowledge them with love, then step around them and get on with living, with no regrets.

Start today to live your life boldly, setting aside imagined fears and embracing life's challenges.
This Week:

Do this short exercise each morning to let go of fears: Sit quietly with eyes closed and imagine yourself taking a safe and relaxing walk along a beach, meadow, forest, wherever your mind desires. Be aware of the sounds, scents, smells, and feelings of your lovely stroll. After a bit, stop on your path and let your mind think of a fear you grapple with. Really feel that fear, as you rest in safety, and note where it resides in your body. Imagine drawing the energy of that fear out of your body and cupping it in your hands. Say to it, "Thank you for trying to protect me, but I no longer need you, and I let you go." Now, drop that fear out of your hands onto the side of the path. Turn and walk on, as the fear dissolves into the earth behind you. Continue your walk, feeling yourself light, liberated and joyful after shedding the fear. When ready, open your eyes and start your day with fearlessness. Write in your journal about the fear you released, then make a list of some things you can do now that the fear is not holding you back.

Ongoing Goal:

Stop fears of what "might" occur with this affirmation: "I do not know what will happen, but whatever happens, I know that I will deal with it capably."

- the ability to take a deep breath
- men who see beauty in every woman
- BONES TO HOLD ME UP
- a warm blanket at night
- OLD FRIENDS
- the sky
- HOPE
- fog in a valley
- kitties
- SLEEP
- COLORS
- family
- BATHS
- hummingbirds on treetops
- stillness
- People who hurt yet keep hoping
- laughter at unexpected moments
- Band-Aids
- SUNSETS and sunrises
- actual freedom
- frogs croaking in fields
- birds singing
- my skin
- Sirens. Because someone is saving someone
- BRIDGES
- people who smile at you in passing
- the hair on my body

Week Seven

G is for Gratitude

Daily Reminder

"I am grateful for what I have today. I will live this day with full appreciation for everything in it."

Gratitude is the portal to everything

Developing a daily gratitude habit is probably the easiest way to improve your life.

Gratitude leads the way to abundance, happiness, success, joy, and so much more. Practicing being grateful has been shown to improve one's physical, emotional, and even social lives.

It is easy to hinge gratitude on getting the things we want (we are thankful when we get a bigger house or a better job or a win of some sort), but blessings come when we make gratitude the platform for all that we have, right here and now.

Being grateful for our situation can be difficult when we are surrounded by the glorification of consumerism and ego. Our society heaps admiration on people who are rich, famous, beautiful, high-achieving. We can feel despondent when, by comparison, we feel we lack these things. Remind yourself that there will always be people who have more and people who have less. The road to happiness is not lined with feelings of envy or superiority; the road to happiness is paved in gold with recognition and appreciation for what you have in your life at this moment.

Many people learn gratitude the hard way: "It wasn't until I lost everything that I realized how much I had to be grateful for." Stories abound of people who are at the very end of their rope but find their way back, stronger than ever. How? By being grateful for the rope. And grateful for the hands that can still hang on to the rope. And grateful for the muscles that can pull you up the rope. And grateful for the pallet that you flop onto when you mount the rope. No matter how tough life is, there is always room for gratitude. And, if you are already at the top of your rope, remember to be grateful for the gifts that got you there.

Gratitude is a high-frequency emotion and, as such, it will attract people, circumstances, and things that are also at a high frequency.

Start today to practice the *gratitude-attitude* and watch as your life blossoms in new ways.

This Week:

Place a notebook by your bedside. Every night before you go to bed, write down something for which you are grateful, no matter how small. Take a moment to close your eyes and really feel the gratitude fill your soul. Repeat in the morning, to start your day with a grateful attitude.

Ongoing Goal:

Imagine you carry a gratitude bowl with you always. Any time you feel irritated, worried, or depressed, stop to peer into your bowl and focus on something to be grateful for, in your life, or in the situation of the moment.

Quell not the
bubbles
that rise within you
-

Tether them like
balloons
and ride them to
the sky
until you can see
beyond the horizon

-Cate Schultz

Week Eight

H is for Hope

Daily Reminder

"No matter what happened in the past, or how I feel now, hope is always available to me. I choose to allow myself to float along the river of life buoyed by the hope of what lies ahead."

Hope is always available for us to choose

The saying "Hope Springs Eternal" indicates that no matter how bad things may seem, we have continuous access to an internal spring, or fountain, of hope. The water analogy is very apt for hope. Life itself is like a river: sometimes the water goes up; sometimes the water goes down, sometimes there is a rocky stretch; other times are calm, turbulent, or have backward eddies. Allowing ourselves to "go with the flow" and not trying to fight the current takes us painlessly from this moment to a new moment and from this day to a new day, with a bountiful "spring" of opportunities to experience, like fresh flowing water.

We may feel our current situation is unbearable, but even the word current comes with a water analogy of "running, flowing, moving along." Life is always changing, always moving. It is impossible for it to be static, or to remain still. Knowing that the river of life constantly carries us forward allows us to maintain a *belief in better times*. Hope for what lies in the next moment, or just around the bend, is always appropriate.

People who feel despair may be fighting the current, by trying to swim backwards or spending too much time looking back-stream, with the belief that the past is where answers lie. Let yesterday go. Turn your sights downstream, knowing that the new day, with all its hope, lies that way. People who feel they are drowning may have forgotten that hope floats. Regardless of the whirlpool you may be twirling in, and no matter how rank the river may seem right now, hope is always there for you. Grab a Hope Floatie and let it carry you down the eternal stream to a new place of fresh water.

Start today to apply hope, at will, regardless of your current circumstances.

This Week:

Hope floats in us, if we allow it. Each morning, take a few minutes to stand in front of the mirror and say, "I have an unlimited supply of hope." Close your eyes and imagine that you have an unquenchable spring of fresh clear water that bubbles up within you like a fountain, providing a life-giving source of hope. Now decide on one little thing you can do today that will direct your course to a better place downstream. Don't think you have to change your whole world; just change one thing for today. Maybe you can go for a short walk. Or hug your teenager. Or skip dessert. Just today. You can deal with tomorrow tomorrow. Know that one little positive thing, no matter how big or small, will help steer you to a better place. Smile, because you have created a hope buoy. Know that this supply of hope will carry you down the river to exactly where you need to be. Repeat throughout the day as needed. Record thoughts and experiences in your journal.

Ongoing Goal:

Know that it is okay to feel down, but don't wallow in it. Instead, charge up your internal fountain of hope and float on downstream, believing always in the bounty of life.

The divine in me recognizes the divine in you
I breathe the air
and my heart is full of love-
I hear the truth
and I sing it back to you-
wisdom and beauty
reveal themselves-
I am filled with light
I am filled with light
I am filled with light
Namaste

-Cate Schultz

Week Nine

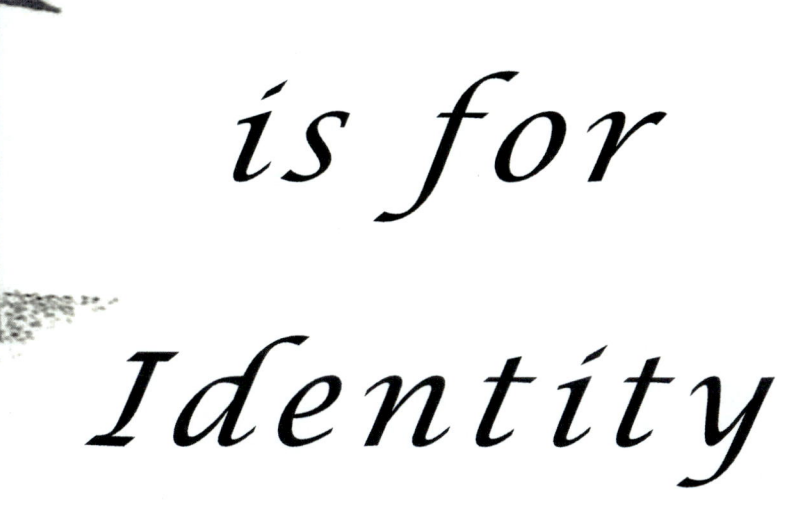

is for Identity

Daily Reminder

"We are each perfect beings doing the best we can with what we have."

Our Identity defines us...or does it....

We all have beliefs about who we are. We are a mom, mayor, musician. We carry titles around as if they are us. And while some identifiers seem inarguable ("Well, I AM a parent"), some are more personality types (I am a high-achiever, an introvert, a perfectionist, a slob), and others simply habits (I am a smoker, runner, vegan, nightowl).

It may seem like the tags we carry with us really do define us. But they really don't. They are roles we have adopted, like actors on a stage. How we *ACT* and who we *ARE* are completely different things.

At the soul level, we are perfect spirits, divine sparks of light. Here on earth, we wear a human costume, modified by the inputs we've received from family, friends, and society. And we constantly qualify our perfect SPIRIT-SELF by this learned behavior. Most tags we place upon ourselves, and others, come with an emotional judgment (good or bad) that pats us on the back or drags us around helpless. Note your reaction to the following labels: Republican, volunteer, doctor, convict, minister, addict, fat, generous, lazy, liberal, forgetful, outgoing, loud, gay, rich, homeless, selfish. Depending on our (learned) perspective, we judge people by these and other qualities. Yet, in reality, we are none of these things, good or bad. We are a human *BE*ings, not human *DO*ings. As radical as it sounds, *who you ARE has nothing to do with what you DO*.

When you realize your identity is separate from your behavior, you can begin to eradicate judgment, of others and of yourself. You are not a slob; you simply choose to not put things away. You are not a smoker; you simply choose to buy and light cigarettes. You are not an overeater, you simply choose to put cookies in your mouth. So, you see, the seemingly impossible task of changing your SELF, or being something you are not, is unnecessary! If you want a different life experience, simply change an action. One at a time. Those tags you think identify you? Drop them. They do not define you. Tags you have put on others? Let them go. Your child is not lazy, your boss is not heartless, your spouse is not mean. When you remove emotion-laden identifiers, acceptance and compassion become powerful catalysts for change.

Start today to see beyond surface behaviors and focus instead on the divine SPIRIT-SELF inside each of us.

This Week:

Start each day by remembering you are a perfect being doing the best you can. Choose one personal behavior you will modify today to improve your experience of this journey through life. Now, think of one behavior someone else does that you dislike. Decide to look at this perfect person, also doing the best they can, with compassion and acceptance instead of judgment. Record in your journal.

Ongoing Goal:

Continue to guard against putting tags on yourself and others. Love who you ARE (perfect and unlimited) and use that love to gradually change the way you ACT to reflect the true beauty of you. Treat the perfect souls around you with the same respect and love.

When you do things from your soul, you feel a river moving in you, a joy.
            -Rumi

Photo courtesy of Joshua Hibbert on unsplash

Week Ten

J is for Joy

Daily Reminder

"Although the people and events of life are always changing, a beacon of Joy shines through all seasons of my life."

Choose to be a creature of Joy

Joy is cultivated from within. Unlike happiness, which is often dependent on circumstances, joy is not contingent on external events or another's behavior. Joy does not require money or time or luck or anyone's participation to exist. Joy comes from inside of us and is there for the choosing. Joy comes in the stillness that flows from making peace with who you are, where you are, and why you are. When you recognize the complete irrelevance of who you are with (or not with), what you have accomplished (or not), where you went to school (or didn't), how much money and stuff you have accumulated (or not), only then can you step fully into joy.

Joy abides. Joy abides in love and loss, in up times and down, in good times and bad. Joy abides in life and, yes, even in death. Joy is really the pinnacle of human existence. It is what you have when you combine hope, gratitude, peace, love. It comes from being present and aware and accepting of what is. Joy is knowing that you are exactly where you should be right now. Your body, your relationships, your job, your living arrangements – they are all perfect, even in their imperfections. And they are where you should be right now.

Joy is not fatalism. Goals and aspirations are wonderful and useful. Move toward them as you desire, but make that movement be choreographed in joy. Know that your current situation is a precious opportunity for growth. Hold your life, as it is right now, in your heart with gratitude and treat each experience with honesty and integrity. Learn the lessons of the moment, and cherish every precious bit of life and death.

Start today to make your life a dance with Joy.

This Week:

Use the Affirmations in the back of this book, pages 115-116, to create a practice of Joy. If possible, write them down and post them somewhere prominent, like the bathroom mirror. Each morning, read the affirmations aloud in front of the mirror. At first, it may be difficult to believe them, but read them aloud anyway. After each one, close your eyes and take a deep breath, breathing the affirmation into your soul. Make a copy of the affirmations to carry with you and use as a reminder throughout the day. Note your experiences and reactions in your journal.

Ongoing Goal:

Continue to make affirmations a part of each day, updated as needed. Post them at work, in your car, or wherever you will be regularly reminded of them. Soon, Joy will be yours!

Loving Kindness Prayer

May I dwell in safety,
May I be happy and healthy,
May I be free from afflictions,
May I be at peace.

May you dwell in safety,
May you be happy and healthy,
May you be free from afflictions,
May you be at peace.

May we all dwell in safety,
May we all be happy and healthy,
May we all be free from afflictions,
May we all be at peace.

Week Eleven

K

is for

Kindness

Daily Reminder

"I treat people with kindness to improve my life, to help others, and to make the world a better place."

Kindness is a gift to yourself

We think of kindness as something we do for others, and often on a merit basis. We may be nice to those who are nice to us, or who, through no fault of their own, need a little help. We are less likely to direct kindness to someone we perceive to be a "jerk" who cuts us off on the road, or a "mean" co-worker who talks behind our back, or a guy who "should" be working instead of begging on the streets. However, science shows that we are the primary beneficiaries of our own kindness, perhaps even more so when we do not really feel like being kind, but we do it anyway. Kindness improves blood pressure and heart health, reduces stress, anxiety, pain, and depression, slows aging, and increases energy, happiness, pleasure, self-esteem, and optimism. Just practice a little kindness and the benefits begin to flow, not just outward, but back to ourselves as well.

In addition, kindness has been shown to be contagious. When others observe kindness, they experience many of the same benefits listed above, and are often inspired to act more kind themselves. One person at a time, kindness generates more kindness, ultimately making the world a better place. Acts of kindness create a ripple effect that positively impacts our own well-being, the well-being of those around us and, of course, the intended recipient of the act of kindness.

Recognizing the obstacles to kindness can be helpful in overcoming them. It may be easy to be kind to someone who is suffering, but more difficult to be kind in competitive situations. When vying for supremacy in a sports game, job promotion, theater role, or social position, kindness may feel like giving too much benefit to your competition. Yet, even in these situations, kindness wins the day. Being kind in tough situations like these reflects well on you, so much more than stomping off the court, or being cutthroat at work, or raging in jealousy. Again, the primary beneficiary of kindness is you, the one giving the kindness.

Start today to make the world better place, for yourself and for others, with regular acts of kindness.

This Week:

Make a list with three people on it: yourself, someone you know, and a stranger. Each day this week, take a moment to do something nice for each person on the list. It could be as simple as giving yourself time for a bubble bath, complimenting a co-worker on their performance, and saying something nice to a stranger in the store. Learning kindness is like weight lifting.
Regular practice will increase your kindness "muscle." Challenge yourself to be kind to someone you don't like, or to give money to a needy person when you can't afford it, or to volunteer to help when you don't have the time. Eventually, the well-being of kindness will spread throughout your life. Record the kindnesses, and any ripple effects resulting from them, in your journal.

Ongoing Goal:

Use the kindness daily list as long as necessary, until kindness has become second nature. Pull it back out for a kindness cure anytime you need a mental or emotional boost.

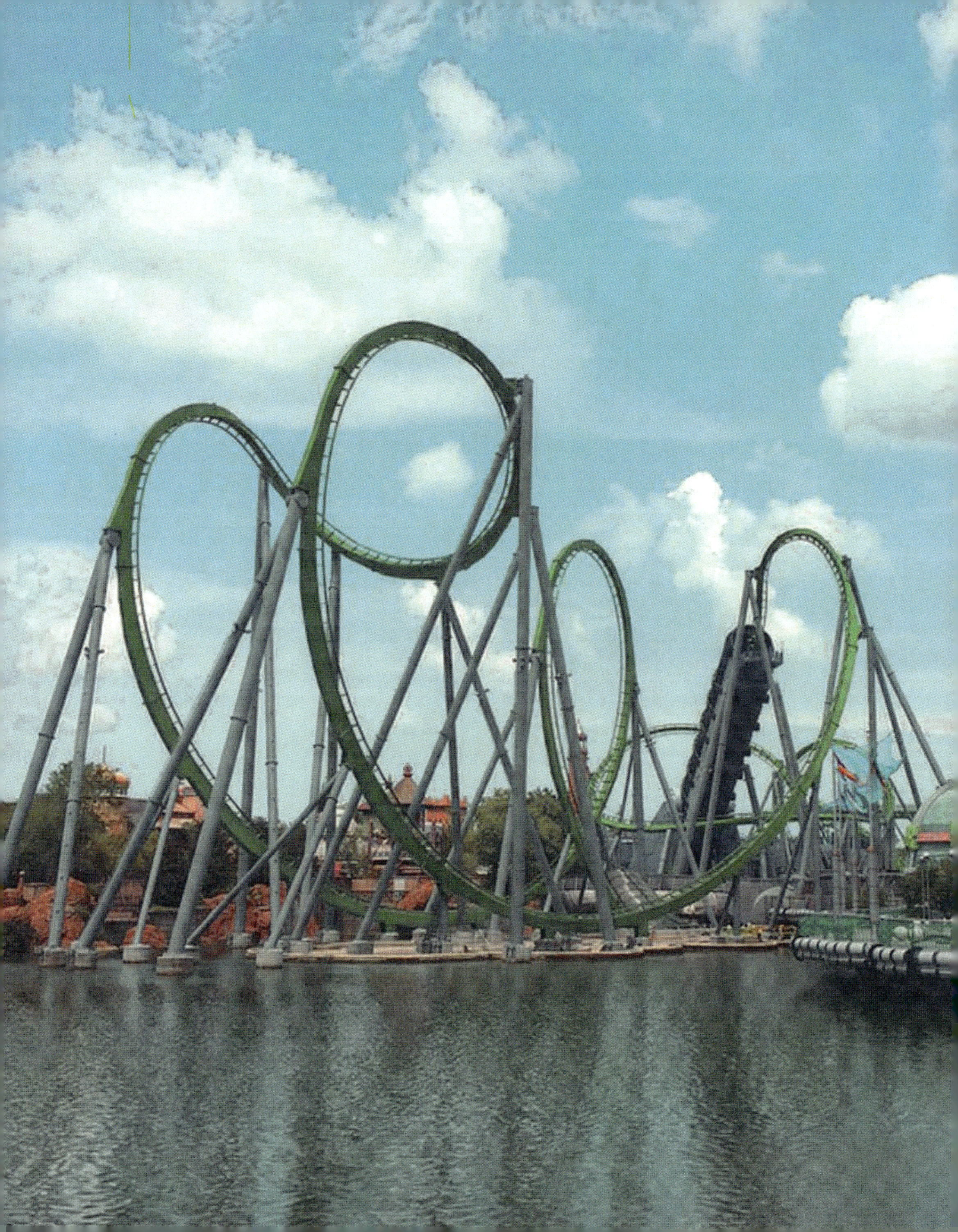

Week Twelve

L is for Letting Go

Daily Reminder

"I am not in control of anything except the energy I bring to a situation."

Letting Go is a difficult skill to master

We humans like to control our world. As a species, we want to control the earth, its resources, and the species on it. Within the species, various groups (countries, religions, families) want to control other groups to be/act/think as they do. Hence the endless wars, genocides, and other violence. On the individual level, we want to control our destiny and we often try to exert control over others' actions as well (spouse, kids, friends, neighbors, etc.). Striving to control is at the root of all conflict, on a personal, societal, and global level.

The hard truth (and magnificent reality!) is that we really cannot control anything in life. We can try to control others, but it is an illusion. We may succeed in forcing someone to convert to our religion, or bow to our politics, or agree to our rules, or submit to our authority but, at some point, it will go awry. There will be another war. The regime will change. Our spouse will be unhappy. The kids will rebel. We can try to control our own lives but that, too, is an illusion. Anyone who was heading down a path and got whiplashed in another direction will testify to the change an unexpected event, such as a death, a disease diagnosis, an economic crisis, or a chance meeting can cause in a life. And that is okay.

Great joy and peace arise when we understand and accept our inability to control people or outcomes. The more we can let go of control, the more we can engage with loving kindness. The freedom of relinquishing demands and expectations is highly exhilarating!

Our need to control stems from an attachment to expectations. We expect a certain outcome from certain behaviors. But the universe, again and again, challenges that belief. We may work hard, yet still lose our job. We may invest wisely, yet still lose our nest-egg. We may be great parents, yet still have a child who turns to drugs. Does this mean we shouldn't bother trying? Of course not. We continue to do our very best, with good intentions, while simultaneously *letting go of expectations or attachment to the outcome*. We engage strongly, while letting go completely. The beautiful paradox.

The only thing we can really hope to control in life is the energy we bring to it. Are we bringing love, joy, peace, and kindness to every situation? Do we arrive open-hearted to each moment, without judgment or expectation? Are we present to the opportunities and synchronicities of the universe, or are we struggling against the current? Are we tied to a certain outcome, or are we trusting that when we go with the flow of the universe, all will be as it should, without struggle?

Start today to let go of the desire to control people and events to achieve certain outcomes. Allow life to unfold effortlessly, in sync with the universal flow.

This Week:

Take time to complete the worksheet in the back, on pages 117-118. Each day focus on an item on your list, and practice the Master steps to relinquishing control. Remind yourself as needed throughout the day that the emotion you are seeking is available to you regardless of outcomes.

Ongoing Goal:

Learn to recognize when you are striving to control, by paying attention to your feelings. If you are feeling irritated or angry or frustrated, ask what unmet expectation underlies the emotion. Consciously let go of the expectation and allow peace to take its place, accepting what is in this moment.

A Meditation Dream

As I close my eyes,
the great reaches of All
cover me like a blanket of snow,
without temperature,
light, bright, soft as night
I lay
lengthened, extended, blended,
into the white
into the silence
into the nothing and part of the everything,
and beneath the snow runs a river
the length and breadth of all things
and into that river I flow,
my hair the reeds on the banks,
my limbs the trees leaning, sighing, singing their own stream
a formless dream, I float,
and my hair spreads
into the grassy plains,
my knees grow mountains,
each toe forming canyons
features evolve, dissolve, decay
and my breath, the river's steam and spray,
creates clouds and washes it all away
into the blue of the sea
where every pore is a grain of sand
and every thought a creature named man
'round I wrap,
an infinite second,
a moment, a whisper, a wind, an inferno
until nothing is left
in the empty eternal
but time
and space
and the surprise
of me,
as I open my eyes.

Cate Schultz

Week Thirteen

M is for Meditation

Daily Reminder

"I can quiet my mind and soul at any time through mindfulness and meditation."

Meditation will change your life... it's that simple

Stories abound of people who have experienced the healing benefits of meditation, and modern science now supports the age-old practice of meditating for physical, mental, and emotional health. Studies show that meditation can lead to improved cardiovascular and immune health, an increase in the brain's gray matter, and a greater sense of happiness and peace.

There are many ways to meditate. It doesn't matter if you have never tried it, or maybe tried but felt unsuccessful. Meditation is a journey. You start somewhere and go from there. There is no right or wrong. All efforts are worthy.

Start today to add meditation to your routine.
Start with the simple meditation below, and learn different methods as your heart directs.
1. Sit or lie in comfort (loose clothing, straight spine) and quiet, with eyes closed.
2. Become aware of your breath, in and out, in and out. With each inhale, silently say, "I am" and with each exhale think, "I let go". Repeat for several minutes.
3. Thoughts will want to pop into your head. That is okay. Imagine yourself at the center of a wheel. You are the hub around which the wheel turns. As a thought appears, acknowledge it and "spoke" it (think of a bicycle wheel with spokes) out to the perimeter of the wheel. Thoughts tend to resist being dismissed, but they are often willing to wait for you if they know they still are attached. Send the thought out and return to center.
4. With eyes still closed, and breathing relaxed, put your mind's eye on something in your vicinity. A tree, a picture, anything. Draw all of your focus to that item, becoming completely aware of it, and only it. After a moment, without changing your focus on the item, expand your focus to include things around it – walls, bushes, roads, etc. Continue to focus on the item while gradually expanding your focus, incrementally, to include an ever-larger area: the town, country, continent, earth, sky, stars, galaxy. Take your time with this process. Eventually your focus is expanded to include All - the Universe. Rest in that state for as long as you like, focused, yet expanded. Ideas or visions may flicker into your mind. Let them float by. When you are ready, gradually return your focus back to your own physical body. Become aware of your hands, feet, face. Allow yourself to return to regular consciousness. You may feel relaxed and calm.

This week:
Set aside 20 minutes each morning to prepare, breathe, meditate, return, and record your experience. Do this when your mind is not cluttered with emails or social media. Your actual time in meditation may only be a few minutes. That is okay. Be accepting of your efforts and open to however it feels. Write about your experiences and write or draw any thoughts/visions you had in your journal. Wonderful inspirations can stem from our meditations.

Ongoing Goal:

Develop a meditation practice of one to two 20-minute sessions daily. Eventually, you will be able to use these calming techniques (breathing, focus, imagery) throughout the day to improve the quality of all you do and experience.

She Became The Sky

When she lay down
in the deep green grass,
she became the sky -

every flying bird
every falling leaf
every white cloud
every drop of rain
every splash of surf
every spark of fire
every star's twinkle
every word spoken
every tear formed
every woman's sigh
every forest's stillness

- when she lay down
in the deep green grass
she became the sky

-Cate Schultz

Week Fourteen

N is for Nature

Daily Reminder

"I take time each day to immerse myself in nature as a tonic to my soul and a grounding to my body."

Nature nourishes our bodies and souls

Most of us spend the bulk of our lives separated from nature. We live in houses that provide barriers to the outdoors; we go from our walled home to our metal cars; from our metal cars, we go to an enclosed office or warehouse; from our workspace, we go back to our car and back to the confinement of our home, perhaps with a stop at the gym or a store along the way. We spend our days enclosed in structures, under fluorescent and artificial lighting. If we do walk on earth's surface, it is with rubber or plastic shoes that separate us from any direct contact with the ground.

Having transportation, shoes, protection from the elements, and a way to make a living are blessings! However, we suffer both physically and emotionally when we go days (or longer!) without connecting to nature.

Scientific evidence now shows numerous benefits to spending time outdoors. From lowering blood pressure, stress, inflammation, and anxiety, to improving creativity, focus, and vision, getting outside is a soothing tonic to the soul and to the body. It is only in recent centuries that humans have removed themselves from the intimate contact with earth that came from walking, working, and even sleeping outdoors, and the epidemic of modern health problems is directly connected to this alienation.

In addition to the increased well-being experienced by just being outside, recent evidence shows that "Earthing" or grounding our personal energy fields to the bio-electrical field of the earth itself offers huge health benefits to the body. Like an electrical current in our house needs to be grounded, so, too, do our own electrical currents. This means getting out of cars and houses and removing shoes to allow direct contact with Mother Earth. Although there are devices that can be used inside the home to facilitate earth grounding, it is best if you can actually put your skin in contact with the ground.

Start today to improve your health and well-being by regular connections with nature.

<u>This Week:</u>
1) Create opportunities every day to get into nature. Instead of eating lunch at a restaurant, enjoy a sandwich while walking through a park. Instead of going to the gym, take a hike or a bike ride. Instead of driving straight home after work, take a detour for a short walk on a beach. Even city-dwellers can find parks and beaches to visit during the day.
2) Once a day, put your skin in contact with mother earth. Depending on your climate, this may include walking barefoot, sitting in the grass, or even just leaning against a tree. As you take time in nature, and ground your energy to the powerful energy of earth, observe how you feel and note in your journal.

Ongoing Goal:

Make interactions with nature a part of every day to reap the benefits of a calmer mind, more peaceful soul, and healthier body.

The Master observes the world
but trusts her inner vision.
She allows things to come and go.
Her heart is open as the sky.

Lao Tzu

Week Fifteen

O *is for*

Openness

Daily Reminder

"I am open and receptive, in mind and heart, to everything the Universe sends me."

Openness facilitates new growth

Most of us would probably say we are open minded. And, indeed, we may be open in some ways, and in some areas. Generally, we are more likely to be open about something with which we have no experience. For example, a person who has never been on a boat, or traveled to India, or played basketball, is likely to be open to suggestions and direction the first time they encounter these activities. However, we tend to develop perceptions and beliefs about things as we experience them or become experienced in them. Sometimes we feel knowledgeable just by reading or watching informational programs. Our familiarity and learning can lead us to shut down our openness to new suggestions.

Although it is wonderful to acquire confidence about your skills and knowledge, it is highly beneficial to maintain a "beginner's mindset," regardless of your mastery in a given area. The minute we think we "already know" is the minute we slam the door to learning something new. The term "out of the mouth of babes" refers to the unexpected wisdom that can come from unanticipated, even naïve, sources. However, if we are unreceptive to new knowledge, we are less likely to benefit from others' wisdom.

Being open minded, or having a "beginner's mindset," is the ultimate in true confidence. True confidence has a grace and humility in its self-assurance without self-promotion. There is no need to demonstrate or insist on being an expert. You just are. There is no insecurity that requires you to disregard others while highlighting your own superiority. You have nothing to prove. When someone makes a statement in your area of expertise, you listen respectfully, knowing that a true expert is always learning and that learning comes in many ways.

Every interaction happens for a reason. Either you have something to teach or to learn, something to give or to be given. Listen, look, learn. Like a beginner.

Start today to embrace openness in all areas of your life, even those in which you are an expert.

<u>This Week:</u>
Think of areas in which you are highly trained, competent, in charge, or in co-existence. Consciously choose to seek input from someone you might not normally solicit for information. Examples: If you are a CEO or manager, take time to ask the receptionist for her thoughts on a company matter; If you are a parent, take time to ask your child how (s)he thinks you should handle a family issue; if you are a homeowner, ask (and be receptive to) your neighbor for their opinion on your property (paint, landscape, lighting, etc.) Each day, reach out to someone unexpected for input. If someone volunteers a suggestion that might normally put your back up, be receptive and open to their thoughts. Record experiences and reactions in your journal.

Ongoing Goal:

Foster a "Beginner's Mind" by posting it somewhere as a reminder. As you become more aware of areas where you resist input, or get defensive, practice opening up to these places.

~ put down your phone ~ close your computer ~ open your eyes ~ listen ~ feel and smell the air ~ notice what your body is telling you ~ lean in ~ let go of any judgment of good or bad ~ just be ~ here ~ now ~

YOU ARE HERE

Week Sixteen

P *is for*

Presence

Daily Reminder

"I am fully aware and present, looking, listening, and loving this exact moment of my one precious life."

Presence powerfully impacts our lives

Being "present" is a modern buzzword sages have practiced for ages. Although incredibly simple, many of us find it to be extremely difficult. Yet, being present just requires practice.

Our body is physically present in any given moment, but our mind is often busy fretting over the past or worrying about the future. However, we have no control over the past (it is done) or the future (it is unknowable). The only moment we can hope to influence is this moment, now. It is fine to enjoy memories and reflect on past experiences or to look forward to the future and make plans for it. Like climbing a mountain, we glance down to note where we have been, and we gaze up to note where we want to go. Yet, most importantly, we pay close attention to each step as we are making it.

Listen to what is happening now. Look at who you are with now. Relish what you are experiencing now. This moment, now, is the only one we can truly live to fullness. Living to fullness may suggest we should cram more "living" into each second, but recent studies have debunked the value of multitasking and now confirm that completely focusing on the single task, or interaction, at hand is most efficient and rewarding. In addition to enabling us to be more productive, being present is also highly magnetic! By being present to the people and circumstances that are unfolding *now*, we attract positive relationships and opportunities that bless this and future moments.

Each moment is a precious and rare commodity and, once gone, it will never come again. The saying, "*Live each moment as if it were your last*" is apt, for it is, indeed, your last *of that moment*. Once gone, it is gone forever. It may be tempting to rush through moments we don't like, such as work, grief, or heartache, but even those moments deserve to be treasured as the tiny gems of this one precious life. Each moment, good, bad, or indifferent, is a part of the story of our life and holds a lesson and a blessing for us.

Start today to immerse yourself in the NOW of each moment in order to fully live a life with no regrets.

This Week:

Step 1: Each morning, set your phone alarms (preferably set to a pleasant sound!) to go off six times (vary the times each day). When the alarm rings, stop and think: Am I present? What is happening right now? Am I aware and awake to it, without qualifying or reacting?
Step 2: Stop and breathe deeply. Focus on the who, what, and where of the moment, without judgment. Are you bored? Stressed? Amused? Irritated? Lean into the emotion. Notice the energy in your body. Where is it? Relax into it and give it compassion. Who is causing the emotion? Open your heart. Move closer to them. Be completely loving.
Step 3: Carry your journal with you to note your six daily "check-in" experiences. Do this every day for a week. Yes, it is a big challenge, but worth it!

Ongoing Goal:

Welcome the peace, joy, love, and health that begin to blossom as you become more present to every moment of your life. Use the phone reminders, as needed, to occasionally stop and ask, "Am I present?" and to turn your focus fully to the moment at hand.

It Is Here That I Dwell

In the stillness of my soul,
where all my cares unfold,
it is here that I dwell.

Where the sacred sound of silence
enfolds me like a solace,
it is here that I dwell.

A unique and precious blossom,
a beauty to behold,
waits like a seed
within
for a quiet moment
to birth and bleed
a blessing to this world....

In the stillness of my soul
is where my story unfolds,
It is here that I dwell.

By Cate Schultz

Week Seventeen

Q is for Quietness

Daily Reminder

"I soothe my soul with regular periods of quietness that open me up to the Universe."

Quietness is a precious commodity

We tend to fill our lives with noise. We turn the radio on when we get in our car and the television on when we get home. We watch sports while we dine out and reality shows while we make dinner. We watch endless news broadcasts and videos of unfolding events on our phone, computer, and TV. We stream music and play video games, sometimes at the same time. We listen to podcasts while we work out and white noise while we sleep. Even in conversation, we rush to fill in gaps with more words.

Science is learning more about how certain sounds elicit healthy alpha brain waves (8-13.9 Hz), yet the vast majority of our daily noise sources produce beta brain waves (14-30 Hz). Beta waves induce biological reactions that are aroused, alert, and concentrated. They also generate anxiety, disease, feelings of separation, and fight-or-flight reactions. Evidence of these unhealthy symptoms is everywhere in our society, a result of our addiction to unremitting noise stimulation, with its potent hormonal cocktail of adrenaline, testosterone, cortisol, dopamine, and serotonin.

Learning to be selective in what noises we allow to invade our space is a topic for another day. For this week, we are simply becoming aware of the need to counter noise pollution with a regular application of quietness. It is in quietness that we find solace, a place to rest our mind, body, and soul. Gandhi said, **"Half the misery of the world would disappear if we, fretting mortals, knew the virtue of silence."** Mandela attributed his ability for forgiveness and reconciliation to his years of enforced (imprisoned) silence during which time he came to truly know his own soul. Modern-day guru, Adyashanti, holds weeklong noise-free retreats because *"all life exists within the space of silence."* Studies show that even two-minute quiet pauses are beneficial. In our busy world, where we are constantly barraged by noise, quietness is an important tonic to the soul.

Start today to incorporate regular doses of Quietness into your life.

This Week:

Each day, take three "quiet breaks" of at least two minutes in length. You may set a timer as a reminder, or just fit them in where you can. If you can't get to a quiet place, create your own silence with earplugs or headphones. Close your eyes, breathe deeply and slowly, and just BE. Be quiet, be still. Listen to the nothing. The universe has its own vibration. With practice, you will begin to be aware of its peaceful and soothing hymn. Record your experiences in your journal.

Ongoing Goal:

Gradually increase your quiet breaks to longer and longer periods and continue to record how the silence affects your well-being in a variety of ways.

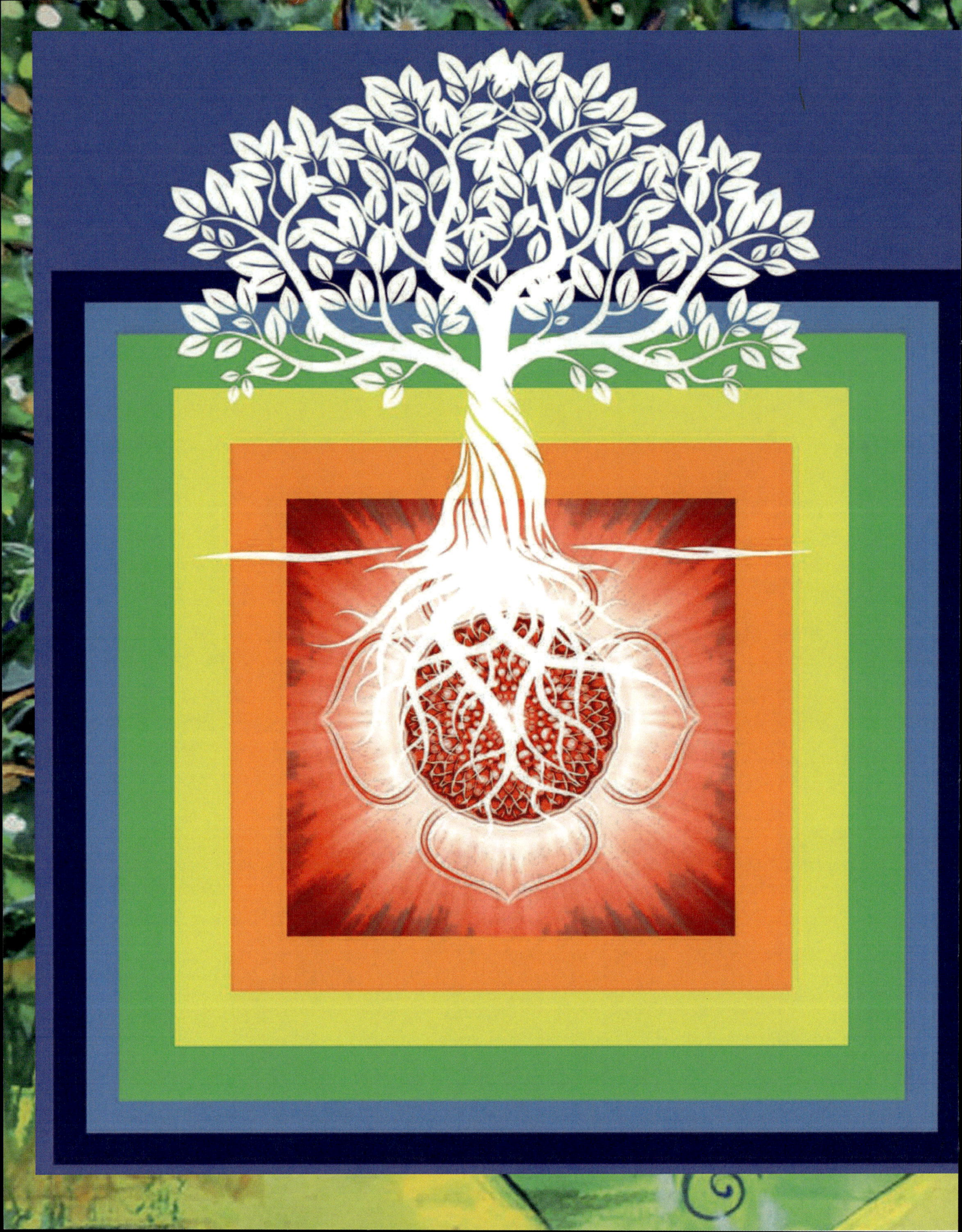

Week Eighteen

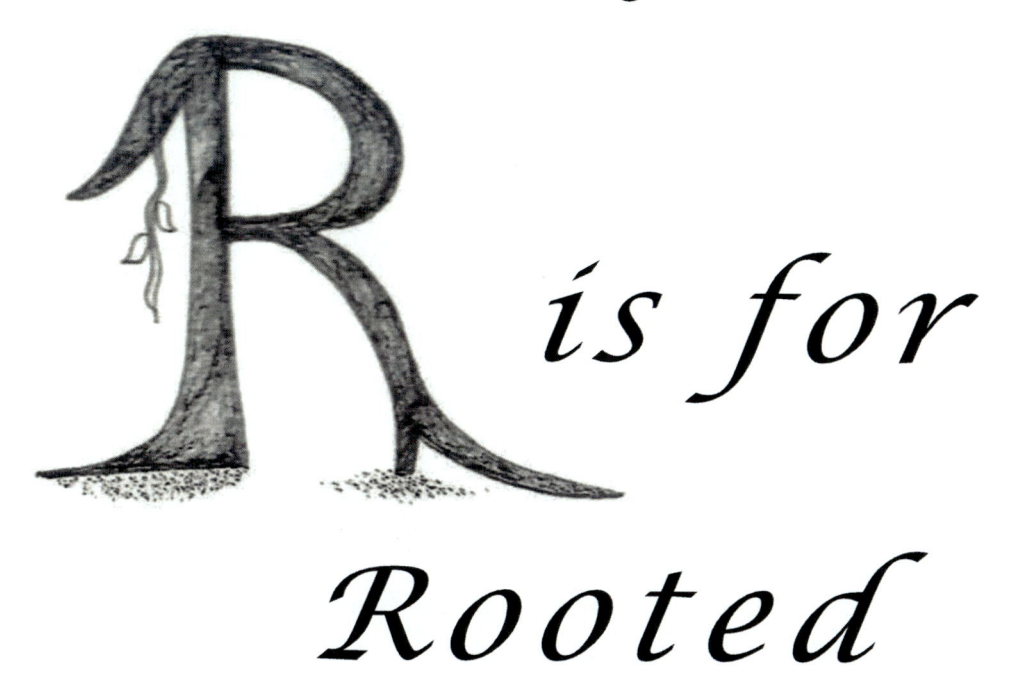

R *is for*

Rooted

Daily Reminder

"I am safe and supported, with my body, mind, and spirit deeply grounded and rooted to Mother Earth."

Strong Roots create a solid foundation

Staying energetically rooted stabilizes and anchors us to withstand anything life sends our way.

Modern science is beginning to recognize what ancient traditions have known for millennia - that all of matter is energy. The eastern understanding of the human body describes the chakras, or energy centers, that gather and organize our energy for us. The lowest of these, sitting at the base of the spine, is the root chakra. The root chakra is the foundation upon which all else is built and is also the seat of our main energy channels. The root chakra is associated with the earth element.

The importance of being well-rooted and having a strong foundation cannot be overstated. A tree without strong roots falls in the wind and a building without a strong foundation topples in a quake. Likewise, an unrooted human cannot resist life's storms, and becomes easily subject to anxiety, insecurity, fear, anger, insomnia, and disease.

Part of being rooted is to know that we are exactly where we are supposed to be right now. Instead of looking for escape from this moment (through distraction, drugs, addictions), we dig in. We go deep. We function from a place of stability and strength. When we accept that everything happens for a reason and that our existence here is perfect as it is, we can know that the blessing of this planet supports us and that we have the power of the universe at our back. We can stand tall and root deeply to weather the storms of life.

Start today to develop a practice of being rooted in Self, in Earth, and in the Universe.

This Week:
Each morning, take a few moments to start your day rooted and grounded. Stand or sit in a quiet spot with spine straight and eyes closed (doing this outside, with bare feet in contact with earth, is fantastic). Start by breathing deeply in and out five times to release any tensions. In your mind's eye, become aware of the area at the base of your spine, your root chakra. From this area, envision a warm red energy beginning to send out roots, traveling down your legs, out the soles of your feet, and into Mother Earth. Envision the roots extending deeper and deeper into earth, all the way to the core of our home planet. Feel how solid and stable these strong roots hold you. Allow the earth to feed energy and nourishment into you through these rich and healthy roots. Breathe deeply and with each inhale say to yourself, "I am safe," "I am supported," "I am secure," "I trust in the process of life," "I am connected to Mother Earth" "The universe supports me" or similar phrases. With each exhale, say, "I release anything that does not serve me." Feel your solid foundation expand with each breath, feel your shoulders relax with each exhale, as worries and tensions dissolve, like rain, into Mother Earth.

Ongoing Goal:

Become aware of anytime you begin to feel unstable (anxious, worried, angry, restless, fearful) and stop to take a few minutes to dig energetically deep into Earth to shore up your foundation. Practice breathing yourself into secure and grounded roots, anytime and anyplace, to keep yourself solid, connected and secure.

In giving, I receive
In loving, I am loved
In serving, I am blessed

Everything I send out
comes back to me,
multiplied

Text by Cate Schultz
Photo courtesy of Ryan Stone on unsplash

Week Nineteen

S is for Service

Daily Reminder

"I give back to my community by volunteering for organizations that help others."

Acts of Service contribute to a fulfilled life

Thousands of years ago, Aristotle posed this most basic human question: *"What is the essence of life?"* And his answer: *"To serve others and to do good."* Since then, countless others have concurred, from Gandhi: *"The best way to find yourself is to lose yourself in the service of others."* to Denzel Washington: *"At the end of the day it's not about what you have or even what you've accomplished… it's about who you've lifted up, who you've made better. It's about what you've given back."* According to transformational change specialist, Tony Robbins, it is in contributing to the well-being of others that we find true fulfillment in life.

There are a million little ways to perform acts of service (one of the five love languages, according to Gary Chapman) and many of us are generous with things like opening doors, washing cars, or making meals for those we love. These acts of service are beautiful and worthy, especially if done with a loving heart that expects no reward.

In our busy worlds, it may be difficult to prioritize something "extra" like volunteering for a cause outside of our own family or circle of friends. Yet, stretching ourselves to step out in service to society leads to both personal enrichment and a greater global good. Not only do we make our world a better place, but we also expand our personal network, strengthening our ties to community and boosting our social skills. We may even gain new abilities that lead to career opportunities. In addition, volunteering has been shown to counteract stress, anger, anxiety, and depression and contribute to happiness, self-confidence, and a sense of purpose. Plus, it can be a lot of fun and even improve our physical fitness!

Volunteer opportunities abound. Whether working with pets, children, parks, or shelters, there is something each of us can do to both benefit our community and contribute to our personal fulfillment.

Start today to enrich your life and improve our world through volunteer activities.

This Week:

Step 1: Make lists of where you might like to volunteer, how many hours you can commit, and what questions you need answered.
Step 2: Make phone calls to inquire at possible volunteer organizations and to ask questions.
Step 3: Schedule appointments to meet with potential volunteer groups.
Step 4: Show up for a volunteer event!
Step 5: Be flexible as you discover different resources and groups you may want to work with.

<u>Ongoing Goal:</u>

Enjoy the rewards of improving your life and that of others by making volunteering a regular part of your life.

howl at the

Week Twenty

T is for Tribe

Daily Reminder

"I am calling out to the Universe for my tribe and actively stepping out to meet them."

Find your Tribe

Being on a path of spiritual growth is exhilarating. You feel more alive, more healthy, more stable. Your eyes and skin take on a new glow, and you may feel as if you are getting *younger!* Love and Joy and Peace seem like tangible elements of your day. You have a sense of purpose and people are attracted to you. Your intuition and instincts become stronger and your dreams may even become more meaningful.

Being on a spiritual path can also be a little lonely, especially if you are surrounded by people who have not arrived there yet. You may find you want to talk about things that matter, instead of spending time with friends who are negative or gossipy. You may lose interest in watching TV sitcoms, or dark movies. You may learn to love a morning meditation more than sleeping in. Anytime our life changes, some of our friends change too. When the elevator goes up, some people get on, others get off. This is the natural process of life. And it is natural to want to be with people of like interests, just as you would if you were a writer, a quilter, a musician, etc.

It is quite important to support your soul with people who are on a similar path. Like a wolf, you can howl at the moon (call out in supplication), and the universe will bring a pack of kindred spirits to you. Listen to your intuition, and don't be afraid to act. You may meet your tribe members in coffee shops, grocery lines, bus stops, yoga classes, or any place people gather. There are online groups and gatherings you can join to connect with like-minded souls. Reach out to these resources for inspiration and to begin using your own growth to inspire others.

Start today to find your Tribe.

<u>This Week:</u>

Each morning, make a simple prayer to the universe to bring you people with positive, good energy. In addition, each day make one simple outreach to a possible tribe-mate:
- Talk to a stranger who seems compatible and follow up with plans for a get-together.
- Call a similar-minded acquaintance and make plans to spend time together.
- Go to a new meet-up, meditation, or yoga class.
- Join an online discussion on a spiritual topic that interests you.
- Make a comment on a soul-filled blog that interests you.
- Do anything that inspires you and connects you in a new and interesting way!

Ongoing Goal:

Continue to expand your awareness of like spirits you may happen to meet, and commit to staying connected to your Tribe, as a support for your personal growth and theirs.

You are known among the stars
You have always been known
You have always been here
You have always been loved

Your spirit dances in the vast stillness
Your spirit
is known
is one
is all

-Cate Schultz

Week Twenty-One

U is for Universe

Daily Reminder

"All plants, animals, and humans are my family, as is the earth I walk on. We are all one with the cosmos."

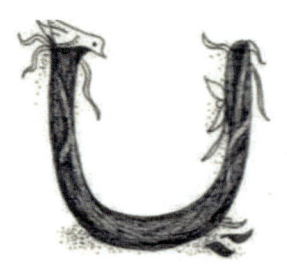

U ALL in the Universe is ONE

When we expand our consciousness, through meditation, awareness, and spiritual practice, it becomes very clear that there is no separateness. Quantum mechanics verifies that, at the core, everything – humans, animals, plants, planets, stars, cosmos, water, space - are all one and the same. It is right there in the name: We are (one) UNI - VERSE (turn/poem/song). Our ego perceives ourselves as different, but our atomic ingredients are the same as the tree outside the window, or the chair we are sitting on. In fact, the vast majority of what we are made up of is emptiness. According to Marcus Chown, quantum physicist, if all the nothingness was squeezed out of the whole human race, what was left would fit into the volume of a sugar cube. Essentially, we are all 99.9% universe, and less than .1% definable parts (protons, electrons, etc). Same goes for that tree. And the rock on the shore that will someday be sand. In a million years, our particles will have been re-disbursed again and again into grass and cows and ocean waves. It is this connectedness that is the source of such strength and power, and the forgetting of it the source of much pain and suffering.

When we understand that we are all one and the same, we understand that to harm another is to harm ourselves and to help another is to help ourselves. As we begin to move in coordinated flow with the All, we find that we have the immense power of the Universe at our back. We start to experience synchronicities (meaningful coincidences) that point the way and pave the path. It is as if the tumblers in a lock have lined up and doors begin to open for us. We attract more abundance, material and spiritual. We stumble upon more opportunities. We experience more serenity, as life's journey gracefully unfolds for us. We have shifted our reality from one of constriction, separateness, and suffering, to one of expansion, unity, and enlightenment.

Start today to sing the ONE SONG that is the great ALL, the song of the UNIVERSE.

This Week:

Simply re-read this every day. Take time to just breathe it in. Contemplate it. Understand it. Embrace it. Savor it. Love it. Know it. Take time to dream about what oneness means.

Each day, make an entry in your journal - Write, question, draw, doodle whatever comes to mind as you let go of any separateness of ego, and become one with the great power and unity of the Universe.

Ongoing Goal:
Continue to expand your awareness through all the tools of this book to an enlightened life, being one with the Universe.

Crazy Last Thought:

If every human on this planet embraced this concept, there would be no more wars (why shoot off my head to save my foot?) no more scarcity (why take from my left hand to give to my right?) no more fear (why worry that my knee might rob my elbow?) and no more death (just recycling).

Vulnerability is not winning or losing;
it's having the courage to show up and be
seen.... Vulnerability is not weakness;
it's our greatest measure of courage.
~Brené Brown

Week Twenty-Two

V is for Vulnerability

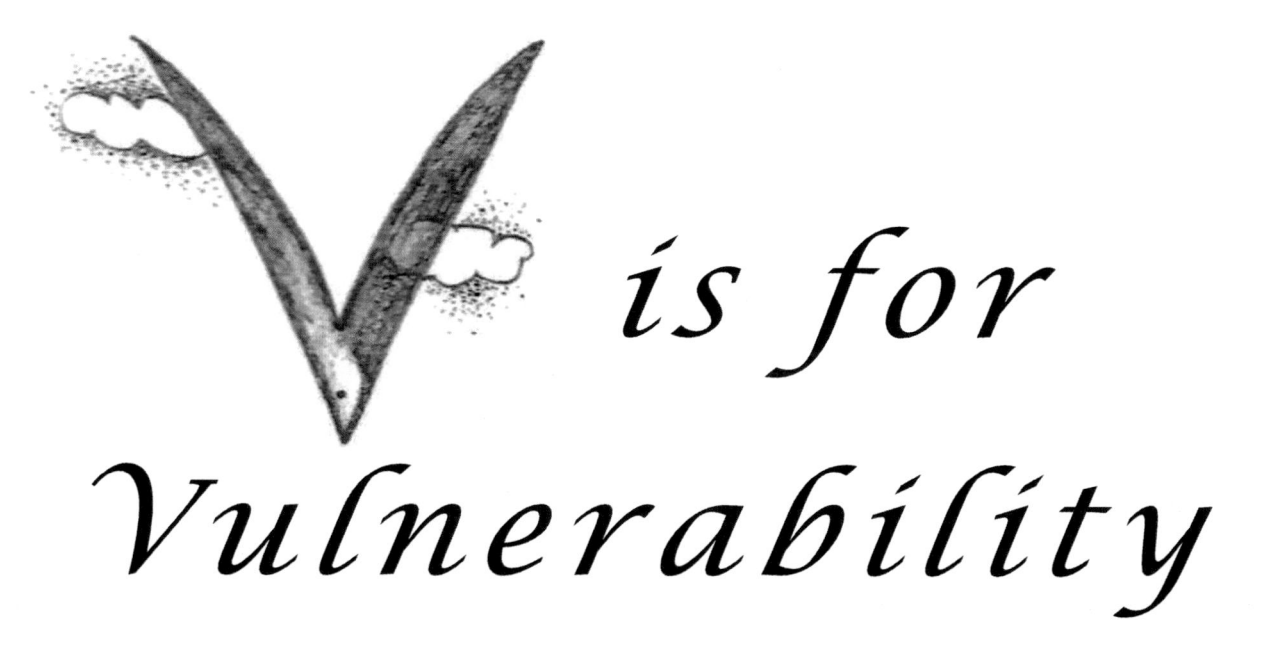

Daily Reminder

"I am committed to being honest and vulnerable with myself and with others."

Vulnerability builds love and connection

Vulnerability is one of the great paradoxes of life. Most of us have been taught the benefit of being strong, confident, and capable. We learned to hide our imperfections or struggles so as not to be mocked or humiliated or seen as weak. We hide weaknesses and insecurities from our family, friends, colleagues, and lovers for fear of losing respect and love.

Ironically, trying to impress or pretend increases the likelihood of losing love and respect. When someone loves or is impressed by the "pretend" you, they don't have a chance to love or be impressed by the real you! Countless relationships, personal and professional, are destroyed by these illusions because lies eventually get found out. "Faking it" - whether it be in knowledge, ability, emotion, or bed - sets up barriers to growth, intimacy and love. It is impossible to get close to someone who is not being authentic, because a certain amount of distance is necessary to maintain the deception. And once the deception is found out, trust is jeopardized.

In contrast, being vulnerable increases connection and affection. Being authentic and "real" is a gift to others that allows them to open up in return. Being YOU, with all your perfect imperfections and all your beautiful humanness, opens the door to genuine love and intimacy.

Know that vulnerability is not a sign of weakness but, rather, an indication of strength. Leaders sometimes feel they must show no "chink in the armor," but the reality is that a strong leader does not hide behind the shield of illusion. A strong person looks bravely into the face of their fears and faults, and walks forward with honesty and authenticity.

Start today to boldly shine your beautiful, real, radically-vulnerable self!

This Week:

Use the worksheet in back, on pages 119-120, to identify areas where you feel fear, uncertainty, shame, humility, dread. Think about areas where you may be holding something back or pretending to be something you are not really feeling. Each day this week, try to make a step toward being more authentic in one of these areas. One way to start a conversation is with the phrase "I'm kind of struggling with…." This is a great starter because it relaxes others' defensiveness and predisposes them to help you. As always, be kind to yourself and others in your revelations. Record your experiences in your journal.

Ongoing Goal:

Continue to practice vulnerability daily and watch as love, acceptance, and authentic connections deepen in your life.

If one drop of the wine of vision
could rinse your eyes,
wherever you looked,
you would weep with wonder.
        —Rumi

Mushroom photos
by
Kennan Mighell

Week Twenty-Three

W *is for*

Wonder

Daily Reminder

"I am reacquainting my Self every day with the joy of child-like Wonder."

Wonder is the secret sauce to a *Wonder*ful life

We all start our lives with the wide-eyed innocence of children, easily fascinated by a twirling mobile, or the first feel of grass on our toes, or the way sunlight plays on a floor. Watching a child's face when they see a bird, or touch a tree, or try to catch snowflakes is a great way to recall what it is like to feel the joy of wonder. Over time, we may become blind to wonderment, either through inattention or as a result of discouraging comments such as, "stop looking out the window," "stop daydreaming," "act your age," and other such statements that scold the wonder right out of us.

We spend years learning to be an adult and striving to be taken seriously. Being told that we are acting "silly" or "childlike" is generally not a compliment. Yet, being childlike is how we welcome the heavenly joy of wonder back into our life! Jesus said, ***"Unless you…become like children, you will not enter the kingdom of heaven."*** We can create our own "kingdom of heaven" right here on earth, simply by re-learning childish wonder. There is no need to suffer a life of sensory deprivation and serious stoicism while we wait for some wonder-filled afterlife. Wonder is available to each of us now, regardless of circumstances. Wonder is found, not in our reality, but in our perception.

Learn to wonder. Wonder at how sunlight sparkles on water, whether it be in the puddle by your door or the sea view from your condo. Be amazed at the way ants crawl, up a tree or across your kitchen floor. Marvel at a new plant unfurling in the spring, be it in your concrete jungle or a tropical jungle. We can truly find wonder wherever we are.

Start today to be a wonder-seeker and create your own "Heaven on Earth."

This Week:

Every day, choose three designated times at which you will stop whatever you are doing, if only for a moment, to look around and find something to wonder at. This may be easy if you are outdoors, and more difficult if you are indoors. Just remember that wonder can be found anywhere, anytime. In a sterile office? Look up and ponder the miracle of electricity. In a meeting? Listen and consciously admire the ability we have of understanding language (that might sound like gibberish to someone else). In a park? Touch and be astonished at the varied barks of different trees.

Set your alarm to different times each day to vary your experience. Be sure to note your experiences in your journal.

Ongoing Goal:

Continue to consciously expand your wonder capabilities each day until it becomes a habit to easily be amazed by the miracle of your life.

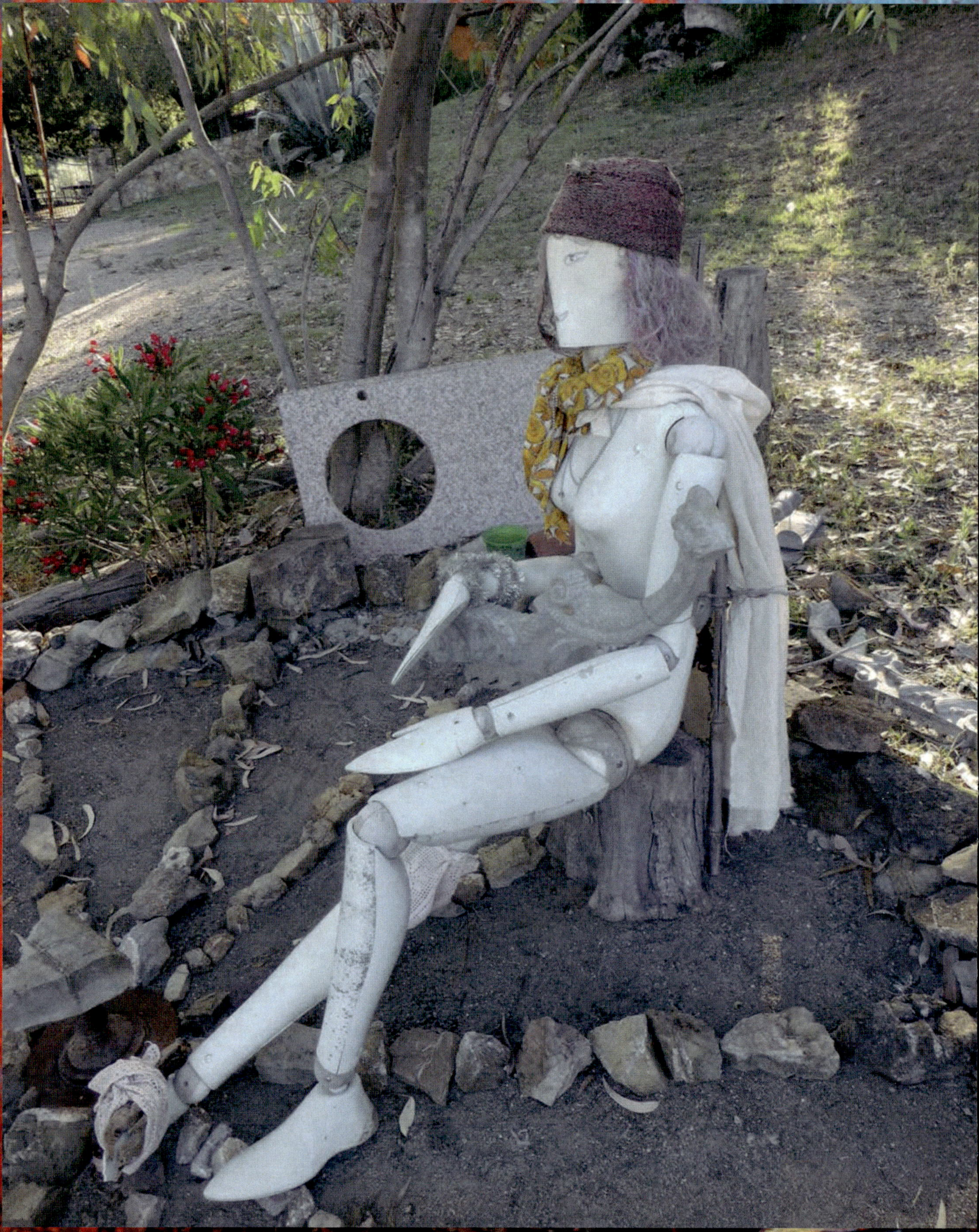

Week Twenty-Four

X is for X-ing Out

Daily Reminder

"I am shedding things that no longer serve me, and surrounding myself with positive, healthy energy."

"X-out" that which does not serve

Most of us have a difficult time getting rid of things. We fill huge homes, garages, yards, and storage areas with material possessions. This clutter not only gathers dust and dirt, it also weighs down our psyche and holds us hostage. By paying attention to energy, we can note how a cluttered home feels sluggish, yet an uncluttered space, such as a spa, feels light and free. Clearing our space allows the energy to flow better, resulting in improved health and a sense of well-being. Resisting getting rid of things is related to a fear of lack and scarcity, with an underlying worry that we may one day need what we gave away. These fears only create blocks to true abundance.

We may also struggle with eliminating toxic relationships, for fear of uncertainty and guilt. We are taught to be loyal and "never give up," which are beautiful goals. Yet, there is merit in learning to walk away from an unhealthy relationship. If someone regularly brings negative drama to our interactions, or consistently sucks the good energy out of us, it may be time to let that relationship go. If all attempts to improve the relationship with communication and counseling have failed, it is okay to let go, knowing that the Universe wants what is best for us. There is no guilt in keeping our spirit whole by stepping away from destructive relationships. Always apply love and compassion, even as we walk away.

In addition, a review of our habits and beliefs may identify some that need to be "X-ed out." We may want to consider whether to allow self-medications, such as alcohol "spirits" or others, to alter our self. We may also want to avoid unhealthy foods that sedate and weaken the body. Another consideration is our regular exposure to dark energy. Frequent ingestion of films, music, and media that promote violence weigh down the spirit. Also, we can begin to become aware of our negative beliefs, most of which we learned from others. Gandhi said, ***"I will not let anyone walk through my mind with their dirty feet."*** Adopt the same attitude toward destructive beliefs.

Start today to "X- out" things, habits, beliefs, and relationships that no longer serve you.

This Week:

Each day, choose at least one item to give away to a shelter or a non-profit organization. Imagine the item carrying with it a bubble of light as it brings joy and appreciation to someone who needs it.

Also, choose one habit, belief, or relationship that needs work. Write about it in your journal as you consider the best action to move forward in optimal health and well-being.

Ongoing Goal:

Post this reminder somewhere prominent:

What I fill my life with is what my life will be full of

Be selective in the things, habits, beliefs, and people you allow into your life, your home, and your heart.

elephant photo from torange.biz

Week Twenty-Five

Y is for Yearning

Daily Reminder

"I recognize when a negative belief arises and I shut it down, choosing positive language and beliefs that direct my life in a better direction."

Yearn with all your might

We all yearn for things in life, whether it be for better health, more money, someone to love, a little house with a garden. We try to manifest our dreams by envisioning them in our lives. While vision boards and manifesting are great tools, they are tools of the conscious mind. And the conscious mind is a wee mouse compared to the elephant of the subconscious mind. To create a fertile ground for actualization, we must recognize and dissolve the subconscious blocks we carry.

Subconscious beliefs are ingrained in us from experiences, often in childhood, that "taught" us about life. For example, if we saw our parents struggle for money and were told we should not ask for new toys or expensive shoes, our meaning-maker (our subconscious) taught us that money was hard to come by and that we could not have the things we wanted. This underlying belief continues to live in us and undermines our yearning for financial ease. Our brain computer stores the programming from these childhood experiences in our subconscious. And our subconscious makes up a whopping 95% of our "program!" Our conscious efforts affect less than 5% of our reality. Hence, using the conscious mind to direct our lives is like trying to drive a train off the established tracks. It doesn't want to go. The only way to get there is to re-lay the tracks.

Fortunately, it is possible to change the tracks that these early experiences laid down. Be a detective, and listen closely to the internal dialogue coming from your subconscious. If your intention is to eat well, but your inner voice says, "I hate vegies" or you want to find true love, but your inner voice says, "No-one is going to love fat old me," or you wish to be healthy, but your inner voice says, "I always get sick," then you have a train going in the opposite direction of your yearnings. It is a radical life changer to understand that none of these things you tell yourself are actually true! They are simply subconscious beliefs, programmed in childhood, that are driving your train. Change your beliefs and you lay tracks for your life to go in a different direction. Be willing and faithful about doing this big work, and you will see the positive impact on your life.

Start today redirecting your subconscious to create beliefs that support your yearnings.

<u>This Week:</u>

Think of something you are trying to manifest in your life. Keep this goal in your mind during the day and pay close attention to any contradicting inner talk. Have your journal handy to jot down words or images. At the end of the day, take time to be still and remember where that negative belief came from. Once you identify the formative childhood moment(s), lay it to rest by stating aloud that this belief is no longer relevant to your life. Then, adopt an internal statement that begins to create a new, positive, supportive belief toward this situation. Use the examples in the worksheet in back, pages 121-122, to better understand these quiet derailers and to begin to do this important work.

Ongoing Goal:

Develop an ear tuned to hear those sneaky subconscious subverters. Stop them in their tracks and immediately replace them with positive phrases that will lay new tracks to where you want to go.

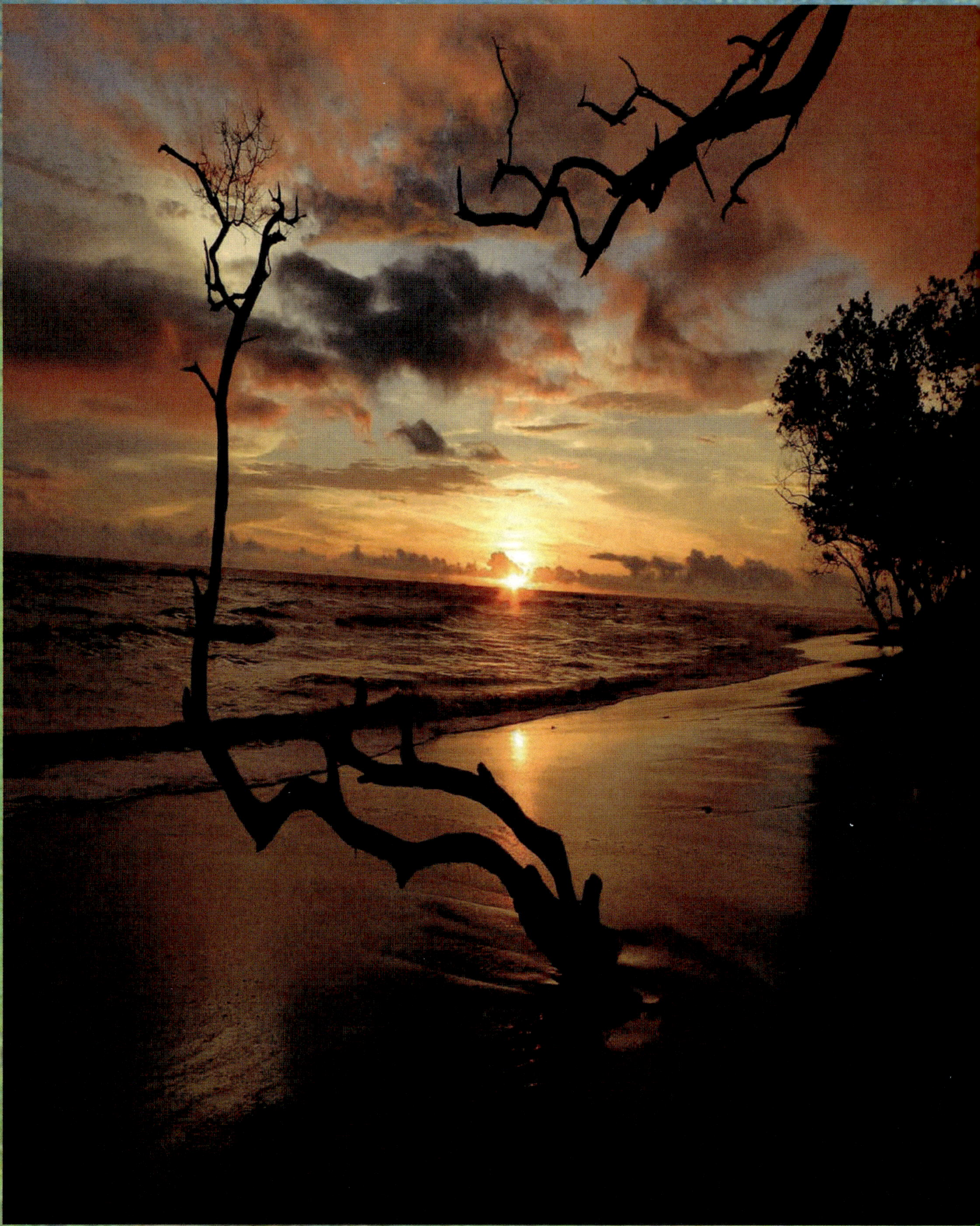

Week Twenty-Six

Z is for Zen

Daily Reminder

"I am committed to practicing the building blocks of living a Soul-filled life, as a gift to myself and to those around me."

Zen covers everything from A to Z

Zen is a millennia-old practice that embodies a way of being, and a state of mind, to bring us into a deep insight of the nature of things, which we express daily, to the benefit of ourselves and others. Zen is about mindfulness and meditation. Zen is about awareness and reflection. Zen is about balance and self-control. Zen is about understanding and divine consciousness. Zen de-emphasizes religious doctrine, and yet Zen philosophies can be a part of any religion. Zen is about being serenely centered through spiritual practice.

When we practice the concepts in *Soul Primer,* we begin to access a state of Zen, where we experience the abundant and perfect energy of each moment, where we are fully present and awake to exactly what is. Spiritual practice leads us to this perfect spot, where we are balanced and fearless. Where we are free from anxiety and stress. Where we have clarity that leads us easily to solutions. Being in a Zen state opens us up to lives of compassion and appreciation and creativity.

Start today to apply all these soul building blocks to every day and every moment and to lead yourself into a joyous, peaceful, abundant, Zen-like existence.

This Week:

Each day this week, take 10 minutes to sit quietly and practice mindful, meditative breathing and awareness. With eyes closed, breathe in deeply and slowly through the nose, exhaling at the same speed. As you breathe in, silently say "I am" just as you did with your *M is for Meditation*. This time, add one of the following words: Love, Joy, Peace, Grateful, Kind, Creative, Brave, Abundant, Beauty, Perfect, Balanced, Divine, Aware, Present, Rooted, Trust, etc. Add any other positive word that resonates with you. If one word feels particularly wonderful or centering, feel free to repeat it over and over. With each exhale, silently say, "I release" and feel your shoulders and your throat and your tensions relax as you let go, let go of the need to control, the need to know, the need to do anything. Just be.

Again, with each slow and steady inhale, "I am … *Love*" and with each slow and steady exhale, "I release." Celebrate the beauty and wonder of your divine self.

This is a great exercise to repeat anytime during the day when you start to feel stressed or anxious or fearful.

Ongoing Goal:

Continue to practice the exercises in this book until they are part of your very being and you are living a balanced, creative, fearless, divine, Zenful life!

Resource Pages

The following pages contain additional resources and worksheets for practicing some of the weekly concepts

Affirmations of Joy
Letting Go Mastersheet
Personal Control Worksheet
Vulnerability Worksheet
Yearnings Practice & Worksheet

J is for Joy

You are the sky.
Everything else –
It's just the weather.
    –Pema Chodron

Affirmations of Joy

I love the divine and perfect spirit that lives within me.

I completely love and accept my body as it is right now.

I adore my body, not for how it looks,
but because it carries my soul through this world.

I am worthy of receiving love.

I accept the circumstances of my life, as they are today.

I am grateful for the opportunities for growth
that this life provides me.

I accept this world I live in, as it is today.

I live every moment with authenticity, gratitude, and joy.

I extend loving kindness toward others.

I expand my life with love and positive energy every day.

L is for Letting Go

Letting Go Mastersheet

Letting go of the need to control is a big challenge, but well worth the effort!
Here are the steps to practice Letting Go:

1) Become aware of expectations you have placed on yourself and others. Use the adjacent worksheet to list things you are trying to control (the word "should" indicates an outcome you are trying to force!)

2) Figure out what emotion you are trying to achieve with the control. If the desired action were to happen, what would it evoke in you? Would you feel more happy, proud, peaceful, confident, loved? You may need to distill down several levels to find the true emotion being sought. For example, "I should lose weight" Why? "I'll look better/have more energy/be more healthy." How will these things make me feel? "I'll be more happy." Write the positive emotion you are really seeking (happiness) next to the control item.

3) Once the list is complete, use it to **express yourself honestly, sharing the emotion behind the ask**. For example, if you want your partner to pick up his socks, say, "Having the house tidy is important to me. I would feel that my needs are valued (which helps me feel loved) if you took the time to put your socks in the basket instead of on the floor." Withhold all judgment or recrimination. Simply speak your need with honesty and love and let the other person decide how they will respond.

4) Choose one outcome you are trying to make happen and **create process goals instead of outcome goals.** A process goal is a habit or a plan that moves you in the direction of what you desire, without pinning your emotions on a particular outcome. For example, if you want to make more money, your goals could be:

- Get to work on time every day
- Apply myself to the job instead of chatting with co-workers
- Look, and ask, for new opportunities to show my skills
- Get extra training in a needed area
- Ask for a raise

Take positive steps forward, knowing that the actual outcome is beyond your control.

5) Accept how the situation goes, without attachment to a particular outcome. Whatever happens is okay. If your spouse continues to leave his socks, accept that you can overlook them, explain again why it is important to you, or pick them up yourself. If your boss is unappreciative of your efforts, accept that you have the choice to continue on, or look for a new job. Know that every situation offers lessons and blessings. Know that each moment offers new choices and that your happiness, joy, peace and confidence, are *not* contingent upon the outcome.

6) Create an antidote to the situation that is aggravating your desire to control, and tie it to the real need underlying the conflict. For example, if your child making the select sports team would make you feel proud, your antidote to over-controlling the situation may be, "I am, and always will be, proud of you, regardless of what you do."

Personal Control Worksheet
(copy this page to use as needed)

Fill in the blanks: Emotion trying to achieve:

I *should* (lose weight, make more money, quit smoking, etc.)
List your *shoulds* here:

_____   _____
_____   _____
_____   _____

My partner *should* (take out the trash, text me daily, make dinner, etc.)
List your *shoulds* here:

_____   _____
_____   _____
_____   _____

My child *should* (keep her room tidy, practice piano, listen to me, etc.)
List your *shoulds* here:

_____   _____
_____   _____
_____   _____

My boss *should* (compliment me, recognize my hard work, give me a raise, etc.)
List your *shoulds* here:

_____   _____
_____   _____
_____   _____

My coworkers *should* (work harder, ask me out to lunch, thank me, etc.)
List your *shoulds* here:

_____   _____
_____   _____
_____   _____

My family *should* (call me more, send birthday cards, care when I am sick, etc.)
List your *shoulds* here:

_____   _____
_____   _____
_____   _____

My neighbors *should* turn off their lights… other drivers *should* drive the speed limit… my friend *should* be on time… he *should* be more attentive… she *should* call me back….

Our lives are full of expectations which, when not met, trigger disappointment, anger, and frustration. Let go of control urges by using this worksheet and the steps on the adjacent Mastersheet to create stress-free and unemotional methods to maneuver life with easy acceptance and equanimity.

is for Vulnerability

Vulnerability Worksheet Part 1
(copy these pages to use as needed)
For each of the categories below, fill in the blanks

My Body:
I want to be perceived as _____
I am embarrassed about/ashamed of _____
I hide/do not want others to see _____
because I fear they would _____
so I _____

My Mind:
I want to be perceived as _____
I am embarrassed about/ashamed of _____
I hide/do not want others to know _____
because I fear they would _____
so I _____

My Sexuality:
I want to be perceived as _____
I am embarrassed about/ashamed of _____
I hide/do not want others to know _____
because I fear they would _____
so I _____

My Skills/Abilities:
I want to be perceived as _____
I am embarrassed about/ashamed of _____
I hide/do not want others to know _____
because I fear they would _____
so I _____

My Habits:
I want to be perceived as _____
I am embarrassed about/ashamed of _____
I hide/do not want others to know _____
because I fear they would _____
so I _____

Create additional pages to explore being vulnerable and authentic in other areas of your life.

Vulnerability Worksheet Part 2

Now use the understanding from Worksheet 1 to explore recent vulnerable experiences:

My Body:
Describe a recent vulnerable experience: _____
How did you react?_____
How did you feel? _____
How could you have reacted differently? _____
(Ex: A loving silent reminder "My body is a perfect container for my beautiful soul.")

My Mind:
Describe a recent vulnerable experience: _____
How did you react?_____
How did you feel? _____
What could you have said? _____
(Ex: An authentic statement such as, "I feel like I should know this, but I don't.")

My Sexuality:
Describe a recent vulnerable experience: _____
How did you react?_____
How did you feel? _____
What could you have done differently? _____

My Skills/Abilities:
Describe a recent vulnerable experience: _____
How did you react?_____
How did you feel? _____
What could you have done differently? _____

My Habits:
Describe a recent vulnerable experience: _____
How did you react?_____
How did you feel? _____
What could you have done differently? _____

Other: _____

Remember, allowing yourself to be vulnerable *allows others to love and connect with you better!*
Check out this great and entertaining animation of the importance of vulnerability:
https://www.youtube.com/watch?v=PJsJ96yyVk8

Y is for Yearning

Yearnings vs Learnings Practice and Worksheet

Our conscious attempts to manifest or make changes can easily be subverted by our subconscious beliefs, formed in childhood. These subconscious influencers are so subtle we are often not even aware of them, and certainly don't realize the power they wield over us.

EXAMPLES:

CONSCIOUS YEARNING	**VERSUS**	**SUBCONSCIOUS SABOTAGE**
"I want to be healthy"	vs	"I always get sick"

(Antidotes: "I never get sick"   "My body is a powerful fighting machine")

"I long to find love"	vs	"I am too fat/dumb/ugly to be loved"

(Antidotes: "I am lovable"   "I have a beautiful, divine spirit that attracts love to me")

"I want to eat well and be slim"	vs	"I hate making/eating salads"

(Antidotes: "I love eating vegies"   "I don't eat donuts")

"I need to get in shape"	vs	"I hate exercising"

(Antidotes: "I love how I feel after a good run"   "I enjoy feeling strong and fit")

"I don't want to worry about money"	vs	"Worrying about money is a part of life"

(Antidotes: "I do not have to worry"   "I will do my best and the universe will take care of me")

"I want to paint/write books/make jewelry"	vs	"I am not creative"

(Antidotes: "I can do anything I set my mind to"   "I am creative")

All of us carry around with us inner voices that subvert our best intentions.
Take the time now to create your own list of yearnings.
(copy this page to use as needed)

~What are you trying to manifest in your life? Write it in Column I.
~If an inner voice comes up right away to cut your hopes down to size, write it down in Column II. It may take a little introspection to catch that quiet little thought-thief sneaking in to steal our dreams, and there may be more than one negative belief we have learned along the way. Write them all down!
~Create a positive saying you can use to shut down the negative subconscious voice and write it down in Column III. Use this positive statement every time the inner voice pipes up with a sabotaging thought.

Throughout the week, be super vigilant for that sneaky quiet voice and stop it in its tracks with your positive phrase.

Column I	Column II	Column III
(Conscious Intent)	(Subconscious sabotage)	(Positive Antidote)
_____	_____	_____
_____	_____	_____
_____	_____	_____
_____	_____	_____
_____	_____	_____
_____	_____	_____
_____	_____	_____
_____	_____	_____
_____	_____	_____
_____	_____	_____

Afterward

In choosing the concept to associate with each letter, I relied heavily upon the guidance that arose out of my morning meditations. In addition, I tried to balance the power concepts to maintain a good variety of experience. Clearly, there are many other practices that could be discussed. In fact, I already have material for *Soul Primer* Book II!

To some, it may seem that I missed the most powerful word of all: **LOVE.** I chose another concept for the letter "L" because it became clear that love could not be limited to one letter, or one page. Indeed, every concept in *Soul Primer* is rooted in a foundation of love, as well as created with love.

We now know that everything in the universe is energy and all energy vibrates at a certain frequency. Negative energies, such as anger and fear have low (constricted) vibrations. Positive energies, such as love and compassion, have high (expanded) frequencies. Love is the frequency of our divine Selves and of the divine Universe. Love is our natural frequency when we are in the optimal state that is achieved through meditation, connection with divine Self, and heart-directed living (as opposed to head-directed, or ego-oriented living).

Our innate, divine spirit naturally longs to exist at the high frequency of love. To achieve this goal, we must become aware of the barriers to achieving love and remove those blockages by learning new habits that raise our frequency.

Soul Primer is designed to heighten spiritual awareness and encourage practice of concepts that help raise our frequency to the highest level. Raising our personal positive energy not only attracts more high-frequency love energy right back to us, it also emanates that strong energy out to the world, positively affecting all creatures, and our very planet itself, with healing energy.

Soul Primer IS Love

Live on Purpose, to Love in Perpetuity

Art by Cate Schultz:

"Unspoken Prayer"

"Divine Soul"

Divinity - "Reaching For the Light"

"Beyond the Horizon"

"I am Filled With Light"

"A Meditation Dream"

"She Became the Sky"

"It is Here that I Dwell"

"In Giving I Receive"

"You Are Known"

"The Impossible Dream"

Unless otherwise attributed, all photos and texts are by Cate Schultz

Cate Schultz

As the eighth of twelve children, Cate began observing humanity at an early age. An avid reader and writer, she has always had a passion for exploring human behavior. After wandering through college, she graduated with degrees in English and French, and big plans to see the world. Her travels have taken her to live on four continents: North America, Africa, Australia, and Europe.

Cate's home base is Washington State, in the beautiful Pacific Northwest, where she raised three fine sons and ran multiple businesses, including a medical equipment company and an FAA flight school. Having started working for the family business at the age of 12, Cate spent 40 years in the work desert before stepping fully into the liberation of doing her own thing. She writes poetry to nourish her soul, fiction to amuse (recent mystery: *Silent Sky*), and spiritual wisdom to put herself out of a job as a Life Coach.

You can reach Cate at
CateJSchultz@gmail.com
follow on Instagram @soulprimer
on Facebook at Cate Schultz - Author
or visit her websites at
Soul-Primer.com or CateCare.com

Art by Susan Cohen Thompson:

- Illustrated Letters of the Alphabet -
- Page Doodles -
Beauty - "Lucid Dreamer"
Empathy - "Facing Edge of Forest"
Fearlessness - "Journey to Thermal Falls"
Gratitude - "Portal Into the Soul"
Kindness - "Sharing Gifts"
Nature - "Bonding With Mojanda"
Service - "Sharing Earth"
Universe - "Multidimensional Flight"
Bio - "Ancient Root"

Susan Cohen Thompson:

Originally from New York, Susan Cohen earned her BFA degree in Ohio and then moved to Boston where she showed her art extensively and pursued her passion by working in art and design fields, as well as freelancing. In 1993, she married Clay Thompson - a Seattle native earning his PhD at MIT. They spent a few weeks every year in the Northwest visiting family and hiking in old growth forests. In 2003, The Thompsons moved to Camano Island, WA.

The inspiration for Susan's imagery has always been a combination of dreams and nature. During her childhood in Queens, most connection with nature was experienced through her imagination and the art she saw in the museums in the City. As a child, she rarely had opportunities to walk off paved surfaces. As an adult, two journeys deep into the Amazon Rainforest in Ecuador in search of an intimate connection with the natural world deepened Susan's perspective of the earth. Hiking in old growth forests of the Pacific Northwest was also significant in forming the basis of her current work. She wanted to take the Shamanic vision of nature she discovered in the Amazon – that everything is interconnected and sentient – and apply it to the Northwest landscape. The moon and planetary bodies have additionally been a recurring theme in Thompson's art. Her quest to reveal the inner luminosity of nature is explored in this body of work, where birds and trees are ever present circling around the moon.

Contact Susan at: susan@thompsonartstudio.com
You can view Susan's work at: www.thompsonartstudio.com

Art by Judith Shaw:

Front (Soul Primer) and Back (Olive Tree) Covers
Creativity - "Queen Bee"
Identity - "Corra"
Joy - "Offerings to Yemaya"
Meditation - "Goddess Dreaming"
Openness - "Seeds Emerging"
Rooted - "Star Tree Goddess Study 2"
X-ing Out - "He Who Guards"
Zen - "Blue Flower Mandala"
"Dragonfly True Sight"
"Reindeer"

Judith Shaw

Judith Shaw, a New Orleans native and graduate of the San Francisco Art Institute, has always been interested in myth, culture and mysticism. Her work, inspired by the goddess, nature and sacred geometry, combines whimsy and the esoteric.

While living in Greece, the Goddess first appeared in her artwork. The Goddess in all of her manifestations (which are everywhere) continues to inspire Shaw.

Judith lives in New Mexico where she divides her time between painting, writing, yoga, gardening, friends, and family.

Judith's deck of Celtic Goddess Oracle cards, a project 5 years in the making, is now available.

Contact Judith at : JudithShaw20@gmail.com
You can view Shaw's work at: www.judithshawart.com

Art by Jack Gunter:

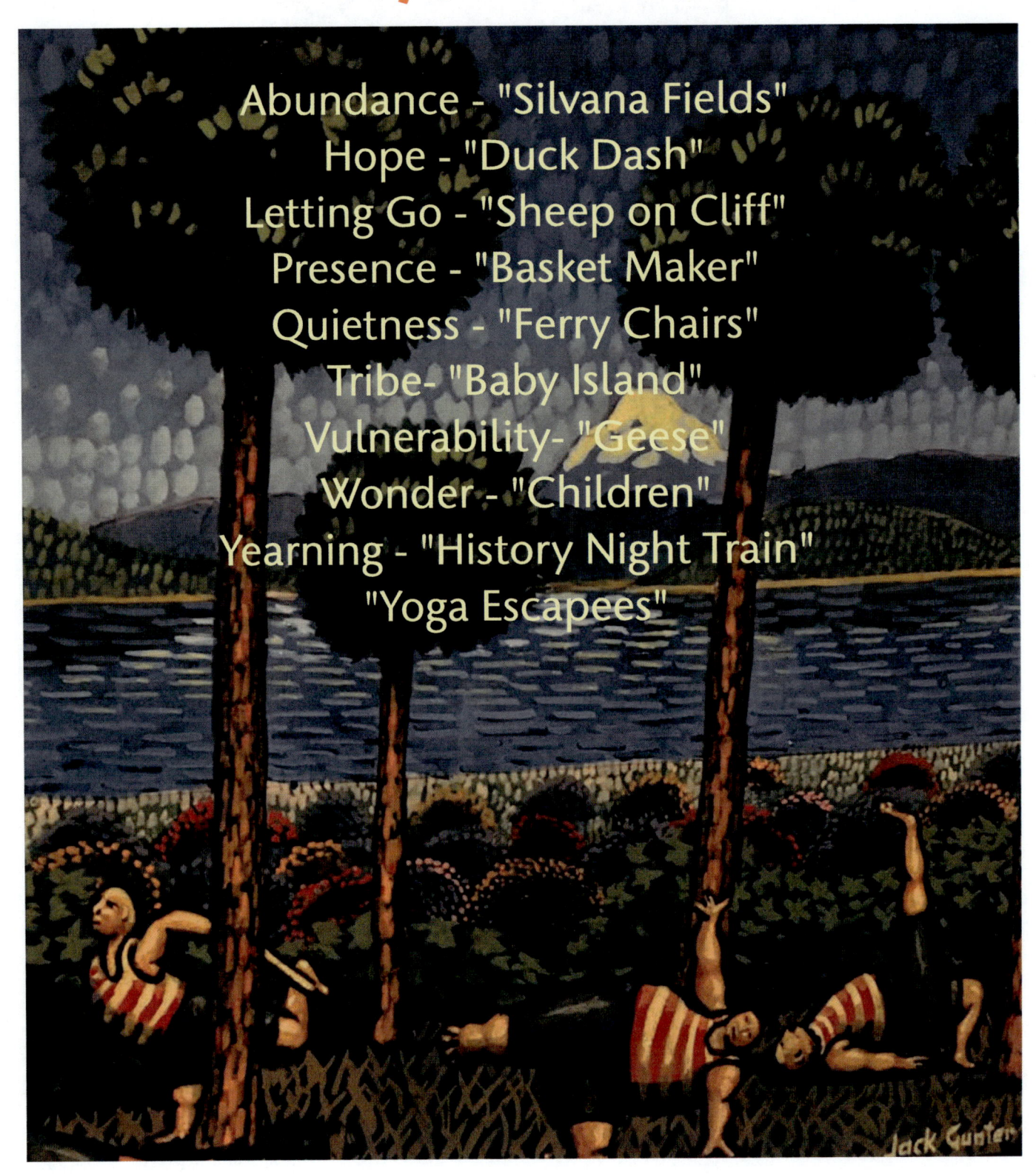

Abundance - "Silvana Fields"
Hope - "Duck Dash"
Letting Go - "Sheep on Cliff"
Presence - "Basket Maker"
Quietness - "Ferry Chairs"
Tribe- "Baby Island"
Vulnerability- "Geese"
Wonder - "Children"
Yearning - "History Night Train"
"Yoga Escapees"

Jack Gunter

Jack Gunter is a prominent Pacific Northwest writer, artist, filmmaker and antique dealer specializing in twentieth century decorative arts, with a degree in biology from Bowdoin College and graduate training in organic chemistry from UNH.

Working as a JHS teacher, he wrote and illustrated his first book, *The Gunter Papers*, a futuristic science curriculum and guide to the fourth dimension, in 1974. The counter-culture science textbook received glowing reviews. Seeking a more creative teaching environment, Jack not only ran the Voc Ed program at an alternative school, he also started a student-run gas station, and taught art to his students. In the process, he discovered he had a talent for painting.

As a self-taught artist, he uses the ancient technique of egg tempera painting and has exhibited his large format works all over the world, including in the Andrew Wyeth and Family show at the Sharon, NH Art Center.

After a studio fire claimed all his existing paintings in NH, he headed west and landed in Washington State with a pickup truck, his dog, and nothing but the clothes on his back. He settled into a cliff-side cabin on Puget Sound's Camano Island, with views of the Olympic Mountains, eagles, and spouting whales out his front window, and soon discovered that the Northwest was chock full of Mr. Stickley's furniture. And he seemed to be the only person in a 1000-mile radius who wanted it! Thus began his humorous Wally Winchester's action-adventure book series built around the dangers of collecting mission oak objects.

Since moving to the Pacific Northwest, he not only discovered a lost civilization, but has also created over 1,000 paintings, three movies as a SAG indie filmmaker, and eleven books, including an illustrated guide to Northwest history, narrated by a flying pig. Nominated for Best Documentary at the Maverick Movie Festival, his full-length feature, *The Quest for the Lost Paintings of Siberia*, documents Jack's recent Siberian trip to track down 17 of his original paintings that had been trapped behind the Iron Curtain for 24 years.

Contact Jack at: flyngpig@camano.net
You can view Gunter's work at: JackGunterArt.com

The Impossible Dream

Who are you to do such a thing?
Who are you to start a business?
Who ar eyou to write a book?
Who are you to form a band?
Who are you to learn how to fly?
Who ar eyou to travel the world?
Who are you to strike out on your own?
Who are you to say you can, when so many others have failed?
Who are you to be so powerful,
in a world of people who have forgotten their power?

Who are you to change the world?

You, my love, are a child of light,
    with eyes turned to every ray of inspiration.
You are a listener, tuned to the whisper of the soul.
You are a fearless star traveler.
    with the immense power of the universe at your back.

Failure is not your fate, for success comes in the execution,
    in the stepping boldly where others dare not.

Failure is not determined by the reaction of those who live in fear.
The only failure is to not follow the dream......

Stay closely tuned to the guidance of the universe and
ask for it frequently, for it will be your north star.
Howl at the moon for tribe members who will support you
and understand that your power, like their own,
is simply a beautiful manifestation of the divinity in all of us.

Never forget who you are, star child.

Never forget that you are here to change the world.

Cate Schultz 2018

Blessed Last Thought:

You now hold the secrets of abundant, peaceful, joyful life in your hands

~

Pay it forward, with love....

Copyright 2020 by Cate Schultz

All rights reserved. No part of this publication may be reproduced or transmitted in any form or by any means (electronic, mechanical, or otherwise) without prior written permission from the author.

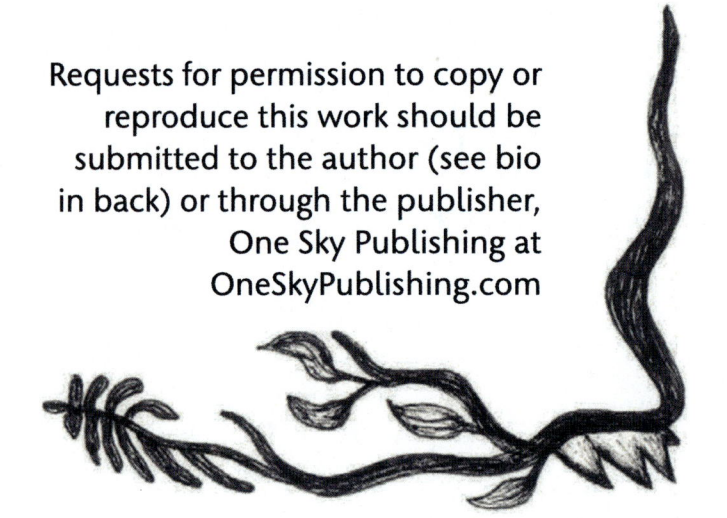

Requests for permission to copy or reproduce this work should be submitted to the author (see bio in back) or through the publisher, One Sky Publishing at OneSkyPublishing.com

Soul Primer Journeyers:

Names   Dates & Comments